PLANNING FOR EFFECTIVE TRAINING

A guide to curriculum development

Prepared by
Tim Wentling

and
pretested and revised with the assistance of
Kah Khee LAI, Yoke-Lim KHOR, Ramli MOHAMED,
Monina ESCALADA and Chye-Hean TEOH

Under the guidance and sponsorship of
Agricultural Education and Extension Service (ESHE)
Human Resources, Institutions and Agrarian Reform Division

Food and Agriculture Organization of the United Nations
Rome, 1993

The designations employed and the presentations of materials in this publication do not imply the expression of any opinion whatsoever on the part of the Food and Agriculture Organization of the United Nations concerning the legal status of any country, territory, city or area of its authorities, or concerning the delimitation of its frontiers or boundaries. The views expressed are those of the author.

© FAO 1993

The copyright of this book is vested in the Food and Agriculture Organization of the United Nations. This book may not be reproduced, in whole or in part, by any method or process, without written permission from the copyright holder. Applications for such permission, with a statement of the purpose and extent of the reproduction desired, should be addressed to the Director, Publications Division, Food and Agriculture Organization of the United Nations, Via delle Terme di Caracalla, 00100 Rome Italy.

PREFACE

In FAO's programs related to human resources development, training is an essential and integrated part of its activities, especially in the pursuit of providing specialised technical assistance in developing countries. Training of agricultural manpower is considered one of the most important strategies for ensuring sustainable agricultural development programs. FAO experts and consultants, especially those working in field projects, together with their national counterparts are frequently involved in various types of training programs, which often are related to agricultural technology transfer and application activities.

Training is an educational process which requires more than just information-giving or skills development. It requires the trainers to have a thorough understanding of the training process and the role and value of proper and systematic planning in it. There is a need to sensitise trainers to the qualitative aspects of training through better planning in determining trainees' needs, as well as appropriate training contents, instructional methodologies and learning materials. Such a systematic planning process in preparing and designing for a training course or activity is usually called training curriculum development.

This FAO publication on *Planning for Effective Training: A Guide to Curriculum Development* is prepared for two major audiences: FAO staff who are involved in conducting training activities, and their national counterparts who will continue to undertake similar training tasks and responsibilities.

One of the main objectives of the *Guide* is to provide trainers with information on how to plan and design an educationally-sound training activity which is based on a

PREFACE

planned curriculum that will serve as a practical guide in conducting a training activity. It provides simple, yet useful tools to develop a training curriculum based on trainees' need. The *Guide* can also help in identifying shortcomings in the process of planning training activities and the possible reasons for such problems, with a view of improving future training activities.

As many trainers are technical (subject-matter) specialist rather than training specialists, the *Guide* focuses not only on the planning processes for training, but also includes ample discussion of practical methods and techniques for improving the effectiveness of training as an educational process. It provides simply-written, easy to understand, and step-by-step guidelines on how to plan, design and develop a curriculum-guided training activity.

The *Guide* emphasises the need to assess training needs as well as training process, including the appropriateness of training contents, instructional methods, and learning materials, in the context of a training program design. In this context, planning and developing a training curriculum become the mechanisms which trainers can use to help ensure the relevance and appropriateness of a training program according to the educational needs of its intended trainees.

This *Guide* was originally prepared by Dr. Tim Wentling, Head of the Dept. of Vocational and Technical Education, University of Illinois, under the guidance and sponsorship of the FAO's Agricultural Education and Extension Service (ESHE). It was then pretested for its contents relevance, process/methods appropriateness, presentation format, ease of use, readability, etc. by a pretesting team consisting of Mr. Kah Khee Lai, Dr. Ramli Mohamed, Dr. Yoke-Lim Khor, Dr. Monina Escalada, Dr. Chye-Hean Teoh and also

PREFACE

Dr. Tim Wentling. The specific and useful comments and suggestions obtained from 60 field trainers of ten countries as the results of the pretesting were then consolidated, analyzed, and used for the revision, of the *Guide*. Their important contribution in the preparation, pretesting and revision of this *Guide* is acknowledged with appreciation.

This pretested and revised *Guide* could not have been developed without the assistance and cooperation of the staff of various FAO's Divisions concerned with training, especially those of the Agricultural Education and Extension Service (ESHE). Other FAO colleagues from various technical division have also provided useful comments and suggestions which have been incoporated in this revised *Guide*. The critical inputs and useful contribution of ESHE's Extension Education and Training Methodology Specialist, Dr. Ronny Adhikarya, who has taken the initiative, and provided the leadership, in developing, pretesting, and producing this publication are greatly appreciated.

It is hoped that the *Guide* will be of use to those who are involved in planning, conducting and evaluating agricultural training activities.

Rome, July 1993
FAO of the United Nations

W. D. Maalouf

Officer-in-Charge
Human Resources,
Institutions and Agrarian
Reform Division

CONTENTS

SECTION I	**INTRODUCTION**	**11**
Chapter 1	**Overview of this Guide**	13
	Introduction	15
	What is curriculum development?	15
	Why do we need curriculum development?	16
	When should we engage in curriculum development?	17
	Who can benefit from this *guide*?	18
	Why was this *guide* developed?	19
	Suggestions for using this *Guide*	20
Chapter 2	**Curriculum Development and the Training Process**	23
	Overview	25
	The training process	25
	Phases in the training process	26
	The curriculum development process	28
	Summary	32
	Additional references	33
SECTION II	**DEVELOPING CURRICULUM**	**35**
Chapter 3	**Determine Training Needs**	37
	Overview	39
	Needs identification	40
	Needs analysis	42
	Job analysis (task identification)	43
	Task analysis	50
	Trainee skill assessment and gap analysis	57
	Summary	62
	Additional references	63
Chapter 4	**Specify Training Objectives**	65
	Overview	67
	The role of objectives	67
	Preparing training objectives	68
	Summary	80

	Additional references	81
Chapter 5	**Identify and Organise Training Content**	83
	Overview	85
	Principles of learning	85
	Principles for organising content	90
	Course planning	92
	Lesson plans	98
	Summary	108
	Additional references	109
Chapter 6	**Select Training Methods and Techniques**	111
	Overview	113
	Determine the general training approach	113
	Types of training methods and techniques	116
	Selecting training methods	133
	Summary	141
	Additional references	142
Chapter 7	**Develop Training Support Materials**	145
	Overview	147
	Types of training support materials	147
	Developing training support materials	152
	Summary	157
Chapter 8	**Develop Tests for Measuring Trainee Learning**	159
	Overview	161
	Types of tests and measurement tools for training	162
	Planning a test or measuring tool	164
	Paper and pencil tests of knowledge	167
	Developing a performance test	179
	Summary	186
	Additional references	187
Chapter 9	**Tryout and Revise the Curriculum**	189
	Overview	191
	Development of a plan for tryout	192
	Implement the curriculum on a tryout basis	198
	Summarise data and formulate recommendations	200

Make changes in the curriculum as recommended		202
Summary		202
Additional references		203

SECTION III — EXAMPLES OF TRAINING CURRICULA — 205

Training curriculum example 1	207
Training curriculum example 2	237

SECTION IV — APPENDICES — 255

Appendix 1: Glossary of Terms	257
Appendix 2: Index	265

LIST OF SAMPLE INSTRUMENTS, FORMS AND WORKSHEETS

Blank Job Analysis Worksheet	48
Completed Job Analysis Worksheet	49
Blank Task Analysis Worksheet	55
Completed Task Analysis Worksheet	56
Blank Gap Analysis Worksheet	60
Completed Gap Analysis Worksheet	61
Blank Lesson Plan Form	106
Completed Lesson Plan Form	107
Blank Selecting Training Methods Worksheet	139
Completed Selecting Training Methods Worksheet	140

SECTION I

INTRODUCTION

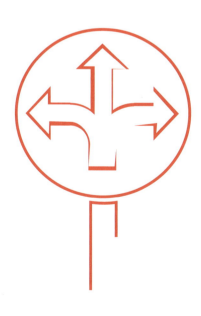

Overview of this guide

CHAPTER 1

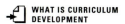

WHAT IS CURRICULUM DEVELOPMENT

CHAPTER 1 / OVERWIEV OF THIS GUIDE

Introduction

This *Guide* has been prepared to assist individuals who have been given the responsibility for training. This responsibility may be one's primary activity or it may be a single aspect of one's role. In either case, this *Guide* may help.

Training is an important tool for assisting policy leaders, government officials, development project personnel, extension experts, and agriculturists in the realisation of their programme objectives and plans. Often, we are faced with the need to change something or to implement a new way of doing something. Training allows us to orient those who will be involved in and/or affected by the change. Also, we may need to provide people with new knowledge or new skills that are necessary to implement a change. Training is a potential solution.

Training, however, is often an underestimated activity. Sometimes experts simply think all they must do is communicate to others and change will occur. Development personnel sometimes think they can just hire a technical or subject matter expert to conduct a workshop or a training session. In either case, or in similar cases, the expectation may be over-simplified. Training is a complex activity and must be carefully planned and implemented.

The design and preparation of training is a major activity that usually consumes more time and energy than the delivery of training. For example, a three day course for extension workers on the topic of integrated pest control probably requires from ten to fifteen days of planning and preparation. If the planning phase is underestimated, training success may be severely jeopardised.

What is Curriculum Development?

The planning of training alluded to in the previous paragraph is what we commonly refer to as curriculum development. A curriculum is the grand design for a training activity. It can be focused on an hour long, day long, week long, or year long training course. The grand design or curriculum spells out the content to be covered in training, specifies expectations for trainees, delineates procedures for covering content, suggests the methods for facilitating the learning process, identifies ways for evaluating or assessing learning, and puts everything in a time frame. The curriculum becomes a blueprint for the training.

Curriculum development is the process used to determine training needs, prepare training objectives, identify and organise training content, select methods for training, and develop support materials for training and trainee assessment. It is a process, and is therefore activity- and action-oriented. The result of curriculum development is a course description and lesson plans. The training curriculum informs and guides the trainer in the act of doing training.

Why Do We Need Curriculum Development?

Curriculum development is a process that makes training, regardless of how small or large, more systematic. Often, subject matter specialists are given the responsibility to prepare a training course or session. Being expert in subject matter, however, doesn't ensure expertise in the design of training. Curriculum development, guided by the process outlined in this *Guide*, can provide a systematic approach to the design of a training course or session.

Experts in training and curriculum development have invested a great deal in learning about how people learn. Additionally, they have studied the best ways of organising and presenting information in order to maximise learning effectiveness and efficiency. For example, did you know that adults learn differently from children? Did you know that individuals have different learning styles? Did you know that using a variety of teaching methods is much more effective than a single method? Or did you know that teaching in a participatory, applied way is much more effective than lecturing? These and other points about training can help us in developing curriculum. This *Guide* has

been built upon the work of these training and curriculum development experts. Curriculum development is a means for systematically designing training so that it can be effectively delivered.

The human resources of our nations, continents, and the world are our greatest assets. Training is a key mechanism for developing the skills of individuals, thus enhancing our human resources. When people's skills are improved, they produce more, are happier, and contribute more to the well being of their families, communities, and countries. Curriculum development, when done systematically, can make the training process better and help us build our human resources.

Curriculum development that results in written plans for systematic training can help to be sure that quality is being maintained. For the trainer, a course description and set of lesson plans can provide a road map for implementing training. This road map will help in keeping the training on course and preventing problems. Additionally, the curriculum can help to assure consistency of training when more than one trainer is teaching the same course or when the same trainer is teaching a course more than once.

When Should We Engage in Curriculum Development?

Curriculum development is an activity that is undertaken whenever a training activity is planned. However, there is a range of sophistication associated with the development of curriculum. Even when experts are asked to make a short presentation, present a seminar or workshop, or give a lecture, they do some form of planning. They ascertain the reason why they are doing it, what they want the listeners or trainees to gain, and outline the event in terms of topics, and logistical details like time and place.

For larger scale training activities such as a formal course, a workshop, or a programme, trainers invest more time and effort to develop a plan systematically. They may have to think about the same elements, but they must think in greater detail and must plan more extensively. In these larger scale training efforts, the trainer invests a great deal of time determining the specific needs of the trainees, preparing training objectives, carefully identifying needed content for instruction, and selecting methods that are appropriate. Ultimately, the curriculum development process results in a detailed course description and set of lesson plans.

The form and scope of training vary greatly. The names used to describe training activities also vary greatly. These names may include programme, course, workshop, seminar, session, or meeting. Within this *Guide*, the term "course" will be used interchangeably with any of these terms.

The important point to be made here is that curriculum development is a necessary activity for any training activity. Any new training activity should use the curriculum development procedures outlined in this *Guide*. Even existing courses can benefit through the use of curriculum development concepts in the refinement and improvement of training.

Who Can Benefit From This Guide?

If you are involved in any way with the design of training, or if you have a responsibility for coordinating training activities, then this *Guide* is for you. If you are a beginner at curriculum development and training, this *Guide* can give you a simple, step-by-step procedure to follow in designing a training course or training session. If you are an experienced trainer, or an expert who has done a great deal of training, this *Guide* will provide you with a systematic review of the curriculum development process. It should reinforce what you already know and do, as well as provide you with a few new ideas. This *Guide* is directed at the improvement of training through more effective and systematic curriculum development.

CHAPTER 1 / OVERWIEV OF THIS GUIDE

This *Guide* is designed primarily for:

- New trainers,
- Experienced trainers,
- Technical experts who use training to communicate,
- Development personnel who engage trainers, and
- Managers of training.

Essentially, anyone who has responsibility for, or involvement in training can benefit from this *Guide*.

Why Was This Guide Developed?

This *Guide* was developed to provide training personnel and others listed above with a *Guide* that can be used to assist them in the development of training curricula. Experiences within the headquarters of the Food and Agriculture Organization of the United Nations, visits with national policy makers, and discussions with national extension personnel have revealed a need for this *Guide*. Many people, when asked the question, "How do you plan a training course?", responded with little attention to methods of curriculum development. Instead, they tended to focus primarily on the topics or content of training.

Consider the following scenario and questions:

You have recently been asked to provide a training session on a topic such as crop storage (assume this is within your area of expertise) to a group of extension specialists in Tanzania.

❶ How would you determine what topics to include in the training?

❷ How would you determine how much time you will need for the training?

❸ How will you derive and formulate objectives of what you

19

want the training participants to be able to do when they complete training?

❹ How will you choose the best methods for conducting the training?

❺ How will you decide on what instructional and learning materials you will need for the training?

Each of these questions deserves a very systematic approach in its answer. The process of curriculum development, which has an extensive body of knowledge in education and training, provides the answers to the questions posed above.

This *Guide* has been prepared to assist you in answering these and other questions as you face the task of designing training.

Suggestions For Using This Guide

Two general approaches are suggested for using this *Guide*: as a learning tool and as a resource. The first approach involves using the *Guide* to provide you with an overview and an understanding of the basic principles and procedures of curriculum development. In this approach it is suggested that you read the entire *Guide* and review the completed forms. This should provide a general understanding and provide a framework for action as you engage in your next training activity.

The second approach involves using the *Guide* as a resource document as you plan and develop a curriculum. As you begin to develop a training programme, you can sequentially review and study the contents of this *Guide*. The sample forms included within the chapters of the *Guide* can be copied and used in your development activity. Additionally, the *Guide* can be referred to as you revise a programme, develop materials for a course, or desire to develop tests.

A secondary use, though not the primary intent, is to use the *Guide* in formal education programmes. Agriculture schools may find the *Guide* useful in their courses.

CHAPTER 2

Curriculum development and the training process

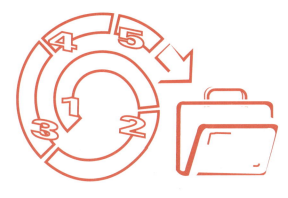

THE TRAINING PROCESS — **CHAPTER 2 / CURRICULUM DEVELOPMENT**

Overview

Training is a term which covers a wide range of activities. The length of a training activity can vary from short term training activities, such as one day field demonstrations, to longer term professional development courses that may last several months. Trainees are also diverse. Generally, FAO considers four main audiences: primary producers, technical specialists, professionals, and students receiving technical education.

As a trainer, you can expect to be involved in training activities that span this range of activities and audiences. However, the overall purpose of training activities and the basic principles for achieving the purpose are virtually identical. Whether you are organising a field day for rice farmers or a seven month-course in on-farm research methodology for agronomists, the phases of a training activity are the same.

In *Chapter 1* you learned the importance of developing curriculum in a systematic way. This chapter first provides a brief orientation to the systems approach to training. Then, it provides a description of the curriculum development process.

After reading this chapter, you should have a clear understanding of the context for systematic curriculum development. In addition, you will be able to identify the major steps in the systematic curriculum development process.

The Training Process

The systems approach to training is a results-oriented process designed to ensure that training is both relevant and effective. Understanding and using the systems approach to training is especially helpful for individuals who, as part of their jobs, train on an occasional basis. It provides a framework in which to operate and a general set of directions to follow to develop good training products. In addition, the systems approach provides you with a process to use regardless of the specific training

topic. This "road map" allows you to be consistent and helps you be effective in conducting training activities.

PHASES IN THE TRAINING PROCESS

In the broadest view, there are three phases of the training process:

Planning. Determining what you want to achieve and how you will achieve it. This phase is essentially the **curriculum development process**, and it includes a series of steps that, if followed, will help ensure a consistent and effective training effort. The major thrust of this *Guide* is to promote and assist in curriculum development.

Implementation. Doing what is necessary to achieve your goals and objectives. Implementation is the process of putting training programmes into operation. The planning phase results in a curriculum. At this point you activate the curriculum. You should conduct the training according to the content you have identified and the procedures you have outlined.

Evaluation. Checking to see that you have succeeded in achieving your objectives and, where necessary, making changes to improve training activity results in the future. Evaluation and feedback should normally occur at each step in the curriculum development and implementation phases. In addition, you should conduct formal evaluation at the conclusion of the training activity, using the tests and other learning assessment procedures to determine the level of training effectiveness. What you learn from the evaluation should be used to identify additional training needs and to make changes that will improve the training when it is conducted again.

Figure 2.1 illustrates the basic steps, and the associated phases, involved in carrying out a training activity, regardless of the length or target audience. Notice that training is a circular process. After training needs are identified and verified, a number of steps are carried out, ending with evaluation of the training activity. The evaluation phase involves a return to the planning phase and will identify further training needs. Changes can be made in objectives, content, methods and materials.

Fig. 2.1 PHASES AND STEPS IN THE TRAINING PROCESS

PLANNING PHASE — Curriculum Development Process

STEPS
1. Determine training needs
2. Specify training objectives
3. Organise training content
4. Select training methods and techniques
5. Identify needed training resources
6. Assemble and package lesson plans
7. Develop training support materials
8. Develop tests for measuring trainee learning
9. Tryout and revise training curriculum

IMPLEMENTATION PHASE
1. Implement and manage training

TRAINING EVALUATION PHASE
1. Evaluate

THE CURRICULUM DEVELOPMENT PROCESS

SECTION I / INTRODUCTION

The Curriculum Development Process

The curriculum development process includes the nine steps of the planning phase of the training process. This *Guide* focuses on these nine important steps. The following description of these steps is provided for you to serve as an overview of the entire *Guide*.

STEP 1.

Determine Training Needs

Your first step in developing curriculum is to determine training needs. The most effective way to determine appropriate content for training activities is to conduct a needs analysis. Needs analysis is the process of determining if there is a discrepancy between desired performance and actual performance of the trainees.

In order to determine if a discrepancy exists, an analysis of the situation must be conducted. This analysis will lead you to decisions about the types of training and how much training needs to be conducted. You can collect needs analysis information from a variety of sources using a number of different methods. Each of the methods has advantages and disadvantages and are effective in different situations. You may find that some training needs are shared by many individuals, while others are highly individual.

Chapter 3, Determine Training Needs, includes a detailed explanation of the needs analysis process and provides suggestions to help you determine appropriate content for your training activities.

STEP 2.

Specify Training Objectives

Once training needs have been identified, you need to describe those needs as objectives worth meeting. Unless training objectives are developed, a training activity cannot be systematically designed to achieve particular outcomes. It has been said that: "If you're not sure where you're going, you're likely to end up somewhere else - and not even know it." To avoid this situation, you must be able to state exactly what you want the trainees to accomplish

and also what you are willing to accept as proof that they are able to do this.

Objectives are statements of what a trainee will be able to do at the end of a training activity. As a trainer, you can observe and evaluate the trainees' knowledge and intellectual abilities, their physical action and motor skills, and their feelings and attitudes.

Chapter 4, Specify Training Objectives, provides several examples of training objectives related to each of these categories of performance. Specific procedures are provided to assist you in developing accurate and effective training objectives.

STEP 3.

Organise Training Content

You should use the training objectives you have developed as the starting point for selecting the subject matter you will include in the training activity. For each objective there is certain information that you can include which the trainees will be able to use to meet that training objective. You will rarely be able to include everything you want to teach. Specifying objectives tells you where you want to go. Organising content into a lesson plan helps you to plan the details of the lesson.

Chapter 5, Identify and Organise Training Content, covers the skill of outlining the training content for training objectives. It provides you with suggestions for prioritising and sequencing content to help ensure that your training objectives are met.

STEP 4.

Select Training Methods and Techniques

Although outlining the training content is important, just outlining content will not ensure that trainees learn anything. As a trainer, you must be concerned with providing trainees with learning activities that effectively present the training content and help them accomplish training objectives.

Chapter 6, Select Training Methods and Techniques, provides you with information to help you develop an overall strategy or approach for conducting the training. In addition, it describes advantages and disadvantages of a variety of instructional techniques to help you select training methods that best fit the type of content and desired learning outcomes.

STEP 5.

Identify Needed Training Resources

At this point you need to identify the resources you will need to conduct the training. You will need to determine what facilities, equipment, and materials are required. In addition, you must identify necessary administrative and personnel support.

Chapter 5, Identify and Organise Training Content, and *Chapter 7, Develop Training Support Materials,* provide guidance in the completion of this step.
Chapter 7 also provides suggestions for evaluating potential resource materials.

STEP 6.

Assemble and Package Lesson Plans

This is the point where you pull together the training objectives, training content, training methods, and training resources into a plan you will use in conducting the training. The lesson plans serve as your written record of how you plan to conduct the training. They will help you stay organised and on schedule. Most importantly, they will help you to provide effective training that will facilitate achievement of the training objectives.

Chapter 5, Identify And Organise Training Content, includes information and procedures for you to use in writing a lesson plans. It provides a systematic approach and format for you to use in developing your plans. You will consider what shall be covered (the content) and how it shall be covered (the training methods and materials) for each training objective. *Guide*lines for allocating time for each part of the training activity are provided. An example of a com-

pleted lesson plan is also included to assist you in developing your lesson plans.

STEP 7.

Develop Training Support Materials

Along with the necessary facilities, equipment, and administrative and personnel support, you will be required to develop training support materials. Training support materials are those things that help you teach the training content and help the trainees learn. Training support materials include audio-visual teaching aids, trainer reference materials, trainee handouts and reference material, and trainee learning aids.

Chapter 7, Develop Training Support Materials, provides information and suggestions to help you determine needed support materials. In addition, guidelines are presented to assist you in identifying and evaluating available support materials and pretesting and revising support materials.

STEP 8.

Develop Tests for Measuring Trainee Learning

It is much more difficult for you to measure actual learning that takes place than it is to determine what trainees think about or how they feel about a training activity. It is important to know how trainees feel about the training, since unmotivated trainees are not likely to be involved in the training and, therefore, not learn much. However, more importantly, you also need to know how much trainees are learning.

It is important for you to check trainees' progress along the way. Measuring trainees' learning during the course of training allows you to make necessary adjustments in your pace of instruction and the methods you are using. When you have finished training and the trainees are ready to return to their work, you need to know their skills in performing all the training objectives. Measuring trainees' learning provides you with concrete feedback about what the training programme has achieved.

SUMMARY

SECTION I / INTRODUCTION

Determining the extent of learning requires that you measure the progress made by the trainees in acquiring knowledge, skills and/or attitudes related to training objectives.

Chapter 8, Develop Tests for Measuring Trainee Learning, provides you with information and procedures for developing tests and other procedures for measuring trainees' learning. The procedures presented are applicable to all training topics. Sample instruments and test items are included to assist you in developing your own measures of trainees' learning.

STEP 9.

Tryout and Revise Training Curriculum

Once the entire training programme is put together, you should try it out on a small group of people to determine its strengths and the areas that need to be revised. Training programme "try out" includes evaluation of training materials for technical accuracy and instructional effectiveness. Subject matter experts should be involved in the "try out" to provide feedback on the technical accuracy of materials. If possible, trainees and other trainers should be involved in the "try out" to provide feedback on effectiveness of instructional materials and methods.

Chapter 9, Tryout and Revise the Curriculum, provides you with the information and suggestions on conducting a training "try out" activity.

Summary

This chapter has provided an overview of the rest of the book. Information was presented to help you understand how the curriculum development process fits into the overall systems approach to training. A general description of the steps involved in the curriculum development process was provided. By following these steps you will be able to develop accurate and effective curriculum which is essential to the instructional and learning processes.

Additional References

American Society for Training and Development (1987)
ed. Robert L. Craig,
Training and Development Handbook.
New York, New York : McGraw- Hill Book Company.

Gagne, Robert M., Briggs, Leslie J., and
Wagner, Walter W. (1988)
Principles of Instructional Design.
New York, New York : Holt, Rinehart and Winston, Inc.

Davies, Ivor K. (1981)
Instructional Technique,
New York, New York : McGraw- Hill Book Company.

Laird, Dugan. (1985)
Approaches to Training and Development.
Reading, Massachusetts : Addison-Wesley Publishing Company, Inc.

SECTION II

DEVELOPING CURRICULUM

DEVELOPING CURRICULUM

Determine training needs

CHAPTER 3

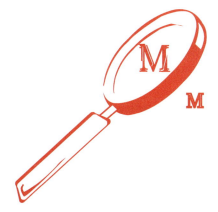

Determine training needs

CHAPTER 3 / DETERMINE TRAINING NEEDS

Overview

The previous chapter described the overall training process, and it attempted to show the role that curriculum development plays in training. It is obvious that curriculum development is a major aspect of training.

Curriculum development provides us the framework and foundation for training. The curriculum specifies what will be taught and how it will be taught. Since the curriculum is so important to training, it is critical that this framework and foundation be systematically based and developed. A major aspect of curriculum development is determining what to include. The "what" aspect of the curriculum is referred to by various terms. It is the content, the subject matter, the knowledge, the substance of training, the focus of training, and many other such terms. Essentially, we are talking about content.

Since content is so important to the curriculum, the process of deciding on what content to include is also very important. The content must relate to some major needs or problems that have been identified. It must also take into consideration what potential trainees already know. Finally, it must be directly related to established targets or goals for the training activity.

The entire process of deciding on "what" to include in training is called determining training needs. This process is divided into three major steps:

❶ Needs identification,

❷ Needs analysis, and

❸ Trainee skill assessment and gap analysis.

New trainers, or even experienced trainers who have never used the procedure outlined in this *Guide*, may find the process of determining training needs tedious or perhaps complex. Nevertheless, as trainers who want to see that the training activities actually solve some real problems faced by the trainees, we have to go through the process.

Needs Identification

The needs identification process can vary greatly in terms of breadth or level. That is, it can be used to decide whether to design a training course or not (very general needs analysis). Needs identification can also be used to identify specific topics or course elements for training. In either case, needs identification is designed to help you determine if there is need for training.

Determine the gap between desired and actual behaviour

Desired behaviour is what we want people to know or do. In an extension education context, the desired behaviour might be: Farmers should be able to determine if a pesticide is necessary in protecting a specific crop under specific conditions. Actual behaviour might be: Farmers are using pesticides at all times for any pest under any condition. It is obvious that there is a gap in this example. This gap identifies the need for change.

Determine the cause of the discrepancy

Presented in a slightly different way:

DESIRED PERFORMANCE − **ACTUAL PERFORMANCE** = **A PROBLEM**

It should be noted above that the end item of the formula is "A Problem" and not "A Training Problem." This implies that not all discrepancies between desired and actual behaviour are remedied by designing and delivering a training programme. There may be other activities or actions which may be more appropriate solutions to some problems. For example, if a government forbids the use of pesticides by small farmers, no amount of training in pesticide use will make a difference in behaviour. In that case, it is a government policy problem rather than a training problem.

People don't behave or perform as expected for many reasons. As a curriculum development person, or a trainer who does curriculum development, you must be able to classify the problem you are dealing with. Then you must collect evidence to help you better understand the cause of the problem.

There are three broad reasons why people don't behave as they are expected. These are:

- They don't know how or when to perform,
- They aren't motivated, or
- They are prevented by the organisation or the environment.

Therefore, the reasons people don't behave as expected can be categorised into one of the three following problems:

- Knowledge and skill,
- Motivation,
- Organisation and environment.

Of the three categories of problems, knowledge and skill problems are the ones usually addressed by training. Even though motivational, organisational, and environmental problems may be difficult to solve, effective training programmes may assist in overcoming some of them.

Within the communication and extension training field, problems are solved through a sequential process. This sequential process begins with an analysis of knowledge problems, then moves to attitude problems. The last step in the sequence deals with practice problems. Any one of the structures for problem identification is appropriate in the curriculum development process.

An important point to remember is that training is not the solution to all problems. The needs identification process should assist you in making sure you have matched training to a training problem. If you don't accomplish this successfully, it is possible to implement an excellent training programme and not solve the problem that brought about the need for training.

Identify a Solution to the Problem

Once a problem is categorised as a knowledge and skill, motivational, or organisational and environmental problem, the next step is to identify a solution for the problem. The solution often emerges from a closer look at the problem. For example, farmers may be losing a significant portion of their crop because they are using improper storage methods. You could easily categorise this as a skill problem: Farmers do not know how to store their crop. However, further probing is necessary in order to determine a solution. You can ask, "What is wrong with current storage procedures? Why are the farmers using their current procedures?

The answers to these questions will provide you with a better understanding of the problem and provide a better base for selecting a solution.

Needs Analysis

As stated earlier, a training need is a condition where there is a difference between "what is" and "what should be." The difference can be in terms of knowledge, attitudes, or skills that trainees need to perform more effectively. These components of one's performance provide the base of some of the training related problems identified in the previous chart. A needs analysis helps to identify the gap, which helps to inform the planning of training. It guides the formulation of training objectives and assists in the identification of training content. The term "analysis" refers to the process of breaking up a complex whole into its component parts. This concept is not unique to the training context. It can be used to simplify and understand anything that has component parts. A policy, a development programme, a job, a farming problem, a fishing procedure, and many other events or activities can be analysed.

The needs analysis process involves breaking down the training problem or need into its basic parts so that training content can be identified and understood. The needs analysis process can be divided into two distinct procedural phases. These include:

- Job analysis (task identification), and
- Task analysis.

JOB ANALYSIS (TASK IDENTIFICATION)

A job analysis involves the dissecting of a job or major work event into its component parts. This dissection allows you as a trainer to understand what farmers, fishermen or other agricultural workers actually do in the course of their work. This analysis allows you to better understand the "what is" aspect of needs analysis.

The parenthetical statement following the terms job analysis in the title of this section reads "task identification." Task identification is just another way of saying "what is involved in this job." The end result of a job analysis is a list of tasks or steps that workers complete in the course of their work.

The term "job" may need explanation. If you are designing a training course for pre-service or introductory training, you will conduct a complete job analysis to identify what is required of the worker in that job. However, not all trainers are involved in preparing someone for a new job. Instead, trainers are more often concerned about training workers to use a new technique, a new technology, or use a safer approach in accomplishing their job. Consequently, a job analysis in this case takes on a more limited meaning. Rather than analysing the entire job of a worker, you will probably be focusing on only part or one aspect of the job. In either case, whether part or all of a job, we call it job analysis.

Four approaches can be used to identify the tasks of the job, and these are:

- Experts identify and list critical tasks,
- Trainers meet with groups of workers,
- Trainers observe and interview workers
- Trainers submit tentative lists of tasks to workers or supervisors.

The following pages present procedural steps and forms for the completion of a job analysis.

JOB ANALYSIS   CHAPTER 3 / DETERMINE TRAINING NEEDS

Procedures for Conducting a Job Analysis

The following steps provide a guide for completion of a job analysis. You may find it necessary to alter these steps based upon your specific circumstance.

STEP 1.
Identify precisely the job to analyse

This may focus on an entire job or only one segment. The outcome of this step is the selection of the job segment to be analysed.

STEP 2.
List all tasks that might be included in the job

This can be accomplished by using one or more procedures. One practical approach is to list all of the tasks that you know and can think of. If possible you might involve others in this step. If resources exist, you can use observation and interviews to aid in this step.

STEP 3.
Verify the list of job tasks

This process can involve expert review, interviews with workers or supervisors, or observation. You can submit the list of tasks to five or six workers (who are the target group) and ask them the tasks that they commonly perform.

STEP 4.
Determine how frequently each task is performed

List the tasks on the Job Analysis Worksheet (see sample provided). Show the list to six or eight workers or supervisors and ask them to indicate how often they perform the task.

Use the following scale:

❶ Seldom

❷ Occasionally

❸ Weekly to Monthly

❹ Daily to Weekly

❺ Daily

45

STEP 5.

Determine the relative importance of each task

Tasks that are performed seldom may be very critical to the job. Therefore it is important to gain both an importance rating as well as a frequency rating. Ask the people to rate the importance of the tasks just after they have rated the frequency using the Job Analysis Worksheet.

Use the following scale:

❶ Marginally important

❷ Moderately important

❸ Extremely important

STEP 6.

Assess the difficulty of learning the task

An assessment of learning difficulty is another dimension of the analysis. It provides you, the curriculum developer, with the worker's perception of difficulty, which may be different from your own.

Use the Job Analysis Worksheet and the following scale:

❶ Easy

❷ Moderately difficult

❸ Difficult

❹ Very difficult

STEP 7.

Tally the total score for each task

Do this by adding the scores for frequency, importance and learning difficulty for each task. Record the sum or total for each task in the appropriate column of the Job Analysis Worksheet. Using this system, those tasks with the highest total scores will be the priority tasks for training - if they are revealed as significant in the later gap analysis, which will be discussed in the next section.

JOB ANALYSIS

CHAPTER 3 / DETERMINE TRAINING NEEDS

This step involves sharing your job analysis findings with government leaders, programme directors, and others who have a vested interest in your training. This step will allow you to gain the perspective of others and to provide a means for involving other people in the planning phase of the training process.

STEP 8.

Discuss findings with key personnel in the training system

The following pages include a blank Job Analysis Worksheet and one that has been completed. The completed worksheet is included to provide you with a picture of how one looks when it is finished.

In the completed Job Analysis Worksheet, three tasks (water management, fertilising, and pest and disease control) turned out to be the priority training focus. Fertilising was selected for task analysis merely for illustration purposes, not to imply it has higher priority than the other two tasks which had higher scores.

JOB ANALYSIS — SECTION II / DEVELOPING CURRICULUM

BLANK JOB ANALYSIS WORKSHEET

JOB: ....

Task	Frequency Performed (a)	Level of Importance (b)	Learning Difficulty (c)	Total	Priority

Legends:

(a)
1 - Seldom
2 - Occasional
3 - Weekly to monthly
4 - Daily to weekly
5 - Daily

(b)
1 - Marginally important
2 - Moderately important
3 - Extremely important

(c)
1 - Easy
2 - Moderately difficult
3 - Difficult
4 - Very difficult

COMPLETED JOB ANALYSIS WORKSHEET

JOB: Rice Cultivation

Task	Frequency Performed (a)	Level of Importance (b)	Learning Difficulty (c)	Total	Priority
Land preparation	2	2	2	6	
Selection of seeds	2	2	1	5	
Nursery preparation	2	2	2	6	
Sowing	2	3	1	6	
Nursery maintenance	4	2	1	7	
Transplanting	2	3	1	6	
Water management	5	2	3	10	YES
Fertilising	3	3	3	9	YES
Weeding	3	2	1	6	
Pest and disease control	3	3	4	10	YES
Harvesting/processing	1	3	2	6	

Legends:

(a)
1 - Seldom
2 - Occasional
3 - Weekly to monthly
4 - Daily to weekly
5 - Daily

(b)
1 - Marginally important
2 - Moderately important
3 - Extremely important

(c)
1 - Easy
2 - Moderately difficult
3 - Difficult
4 - Very difficult

The method outlined in the previous steps is a simple process that attempts to explain a complex process such as a job. It is a systematic approach to delineate the potential focus of training. It should be augmented with the expertise of the trainer and of other significant people. Common sense should be used in interpreting the results of the job analysis.

The result of the job analysis is a list of job tasks. You can see from the example that each task is a complex set of procedures in itself. Because of this complexity, and because we cannot usually design training to focus specifically on such broad tasks, it is necessary to conduct the next level of analysis: Task Analysis.

TASK ANALYSIS

Task analysis is a process that is executed in order to better understand job tasks. Essentially, it involves breaking down the job tasks into their consecutive steps or component parts. Once broken into parts, each element is analysed to determine its relative importance and criticalness in terms of accomplishing the job task. For example, consider the job of farm mechanic. One of the tasks of a farm mechanic is to repair or replace vehicle tires. An analysis of this task reveals the following steps:

❶ Position jack on vehicle

❷ Block vehicle from moving

❸ Loosen wheel lug nuts

❹ Elevate vehicle

❺ Remove wheel and tire

❻ 6. - 12. (Other steps in the process)

TASK ANALYSIS

CHAPTER 3 / DETERMINE TRAINING NEEDS

The task analysis process has two distinct purposes. First, it helps identify the elements, subtasks, or procedural steps of a job task. Knowing these elements is critical to the development of training objectives and the identification and organisation of training content. Second, the task analysis helps in determining the most important elements and steps within a job task. By knowing the relative importance, training can focus on the most important and critical elements, rather than treating all content as having similar importance.

In doing a task analysis you will break down the tasks into components or steps and assess them, using procedures and criteria similar to those you used in the "Job Analysis Worksheet." You will rate the frequency of performance, importance, and learning difficulty of each component or step. The results of the task analysis will be used to formulate training objectives. The procedures for preparing objectives are presented in the next chapter.

Procedures for Conducting a Task Analysis

The following steps provide a guide for completion of a task analysis. You may find it necessary to alter these steps based upon your specific circumstance.

STEP 1.

Duplicate several Task Analysis Worksheets and write the name of the job at the top of each

A blank form is included in this chapter. Each of these forms will be used for breaking down and analysing each of the most critical job tasks.

 TASK ANALYSIS   SECTION II / DEVELOPING CURRICULUM

STEP 2.

Write one task on each of the Task Analysis Worksheets

These tasks should be those identified in the job analysis as having the highest score.

STEP 3.

List all component parts of each task on its respective Task Analysis Worksheet

Be as thorough as possible in this step. You may wish to talk with someone who performs the job, a supervisor or a subject matter expert. They may be in a better position to tell you the major steps in a job.

STEP 4.

Determine how frequently each step or component is performed

Use the information you have gained from the job analysis or consult with workers or supervisors.

Use the following recording scheme:

❶ Seldom

❷ Occasionally

❸ Weekly to Monthly

❹ Daily to Weekly

❺ Daily

52

TASK ANALYSIS

CHAPTER 3 / DETERMINE TRAINING NEEDS

STEP 5.

Determine the relative importance of each step or component

Steps that are performed seldom may be very critical to the job. Therefore it is important to gain both an importance rating and a frequency rating.

Use the following scale:

❶ Marginally important

❷ Moderately important

❸ Extremely important

STEP 6.

Assess he difficulty of learning the task component or step

An assessment of learning difficulty is another dimension of the analysis. It provides you, the curriculum developer, with the workers' perception of difficulty, which may be different from your own.

Use the Task Analysis Worksheet and the following scale:

❶ Easy

❷ Moderately difficult

❸ Difficult

❹ Very difficult

STEP 7.

Tally the total score for each task component or step

Do this by adding the scores for frequency, importance and learning difficulty for each component. Record the sum or total for each task in the appropriate column of the Task Analysis Worksheet. Using this system, those components with the highest total scores will be the priority elements for training, if they are revealed as significant in the later gap analysis.

53

STEP 8.

Review the results of the task analysis with someone knowledgeable of the job

Ask several workers, supervisors or subject matter experts to verify that the nature of the tasks are consistent with the job.

Using the Task Analysis Worksheet

The forms on the following pages provide a blank Task Analysis Worksheet that can be duplicated and used in your analysis. Additionally, a completed worksheet is included to help clarify its use.

The process of task analysis, as you can see, is very similar to the job analysis process. You should recognise the important difference: The job analysis helps us identify major blocks of content to include in training; the task analysis helps us understand what comprises these blocks. Both results are important to the curriculum development process. The more specific we can be with job requirements, the easier our training development task will be.

TASK ANALYSIS
CHAPTER 3 / DETERMINE TRAINING NEEDS

BLANK TASK ANALYSIS WORKSHEET

JOB: ....

TASK: ....

Step/s Components	Frequency of Performance (a)	Level of Importance (b)	Learning Difficulty (c)	Total

Legends:

(a)
1 - Seldom
2 - Occasional
3 - Weekly to monthly
4 - Daily to weekly
5 - Daily

(b)
1 - Marginally important
2 - Moderately important
3 - Extremely important

(c)
1 - Easy
2 - Moderately difficult
3 - Difficult
4 - Very difficult

TASK ANALYSIS
SECTION II / DEVELOPING CURRICULUM

COMPLETED TASK ANALYSIS WORKSHEET

JOB: Rice Cultivation

TASK: Fertilising

Steps/ Components	Frequency of Performance (a)	Level of Importance (b)	Learning Difficulty (c)	Total
Collect soil samples for analysis	1	2	1	4
Identify types of basal fertilisers for soil	1	3	3	7
Determine amount of fertilisers required by the soil	1	3	3	7
Identify nutrient deficiency symptoms in plants	3	3	4	10
Identify types of fertilisers required by plants	3	3	3	9
Determine the amount of fertilisers required by the plants	3	3	3	9
Determine time of application	3	3	2	8
Obtain fertilisers at appropriate time	1	3	1	5
Apply fertilisers	3	3	2	8

Legends:

(a)
1 - Seldom
2 - Occasional
3 - Weekly to monthly
4 - Daily to weekly
5 - Daily

(b)
1 - Marginally important
2 - Moderately important
3 - Extremely important

(c)
1 - Easy
2 - Moderately difficult
3 - Difficult
4 - Very difficult

TRAINEE SKILL ASSESSMENT AND GAP ANALYSIS

Knowing what is required for completion of the job tasks is only half of the information needed in curriculum development. The formula referred to in the needs identification section of this chapter is also crucial in needs analysis. If you recall, the formula reads:

DESIRED PERFORMANCE − **ACTUAL PERFORMANCE** = **A PROBLEM**

Once you know what needs to be taught and what steps are involved in the process, you have completed the first major step in the curriculum development process.

What we have just identified in the previous section is desired performance. We must now be concerned with gaining an understanding of the current skill levels of those who need training. This is very important so that we focus our curriculum and the training on the desired and important skills that workers do not already have. It would be wasteful and frustrating to the trainer and trainees to design and deliver training on topics and skills where the trainees are already able.

The skill assessment process is accomplished through an analysis of the potential trainees in relation to the tasks outlined in the task analysis. This must involve the stating of each task and then using the professional judgement of individuals in determining the extent to which the trainees already have the skills. The procedures and form included on the following pages provide a guide to this task.

Procedures for Skill Assessment and Gap Analysis

The following steps provide a guide to assessing the skill levels of trainees. The process is general in nature and should be adapted to your specific needs and situation.

STEP 1.

List the "steps or components" that were identified on the Task Analysis Worksheet on the Gap Analysis Worksheet (sample forms provided)

You should list the task with the highest score on the task analysis first. Then list the remaining tasks in descending order according to their scores. This will focus your continued analysis on the most critical tasks.

STEP 2.

Rate each "step or component" in terms of the trainees' current proficiency to complete it

This should be done on a scale of 1 to 5, with the following descriptors:

❶ Cannot complete any part of the task

❷ Can complete less than half the task

❸ Can complete more than half

❹ Can complete the entire task but takes too long

❺ Can complete the task within time standards

Your assessment of proficiency can be determined in several ways.

(a) If you know your trainees well, you may be able to give each task a rating based upon your knowledge.

(b) You can interview the work supervisors, extension agent, or other people who know the current capability of the trainees. In the interviews, you can ask the respondent to rate the proficiency of the worker(s) on each of the tasks.

(c) You can develop a test or performance measure and administer it to a sample of the potential trainees. This will provide an accurate measure of the current skill level of the trainees.

This last option, though possibly the most accurate, is the most difficult. Your local situation should dictate which of the above methods you choose for making proficiency ratings.

STEP 3.

Summarise the individual responses and explain what you can do with them

The responses obtained through completion of proficiency ratings can be summarised by adding up the total score for each item and dividing by the number of different forms that were completed. The result will be an average score. This average score can be used to identify the components where proficiency is the strongest and where it is the weakest.

STEP 4.

Review the proficiency ratings and check those tasks that appear to have low proficiency

Low proficiency means that there is a gap between what is desired and what is currently the situation.

GAP ANALYSIS   SECTION II / DEVELOPING CURRICULUM

BLANK GAP ANALYSIS WORKSHEET

JOB: .... **TASK:** ....

List steps and components	Proficiency rating 1 2 3 4 5 (see legend below)	Check this box if proficiency is a problem	Can the problem be addressed by training? If so, check box
	1 2 3 4 5	[ ]	[ ]
	1 2 3 4 5	[ ]	[ ]
	1 2 3 4 5	[ ]	[ ]
	1 2 3 4 5	[ ]	[ ]
	1 2 3 4 5	[ ]	[ ]
	1 2 3 4 5	[ ]	[ ]
	1 2 3 4 5	[ ]	[ ]
	1 2 3 4 5	[ ]	[ ]

Legend: 1 - cannot complete any part of the task;   4 - can complete the entire task, but takes too long;
2 - can complete less than half the task;   5 - can complete the task within time standards
3 - can complete more than half;

GAP ANALYSIS CHAPTER 3 / DETERMINE TRAINING NEEDS

COMPLETED GAP ANALYSIS WORKSHEET

JOB: Rice Cultivation **TASK:** Fertilising

List steps and components	Proficiency rating 1 2 3 4 5 (see legend below)	Check this box if proficiency is a problem	Can the problem be addressed by training? If so, check box
Identify nutrient deficiency symptoms in plants	1 [2] 3 4 5	[X]	[X]
Identify types of fertilisers required by plants	1 2 3 [4] 5	[ ]	[ ]
Determine amount of fertilisers required by plants	[1] 2 3 4 5	[X]	[X]
Determine time of application	1 2 3 4 [5]	[ ]	[ ]
Apply fertilisers	1 2 3 [4] 5	[ ]	[ ]
Identify types of basal fertilisers for soil	1 2 3 4 [5]	[ ]	[ ]
Determine amount of f fertilisers required for soil	[1] 2 3 4 5	[X]	[X]
Obtain fertilisers at appropriate time	1 [2] 3 4 5	[X]	[X]
Collect soil samples for analysis	1 [2] 3 4 5	[X]	[X]

Legend: 1 - cannot complete any part of the task; 4 - can complete the entire task, but takes too long;
2 - can complete less than half the task; 5 - can complete the task within time standards
3 - can complete more than half;

STEP 5.

Determine whether the gap can be decreased or removed through training

Not all deficiencies can be corrected by training. This step provides a check and balance against assuming that the training programme can and should include every task that has a gap. For example, if a task requires that a complex chemical analysis be completed, it is very possible that training will not be effective. This task requires general ability in science; it requires sophisticated apparatus, and it requires controlled conditions. If these needs are not allowed for, training will not be an appropriate nor effective solution for closing the proficiency gap.

STEP 6.

Discuss the results of the gap analysis (the proficiency ratings and the indications of gaps) with one or more key people in the training activity

This might involve extension experts or subject matter experts who have a stake in the training. The purpose of discussing the results with someone else is to provide another perspective to the training needs assessment process. Sometimes, as a curriculum developer, we become too involved or so close to the situation that we miss an obvious or important aspect of the process.

Summary

This chapter has provided an overview of the needs identification and analysis process. The process begins with the identification of a training need. sometimes, the training need is already specified for the curriculum developer; whereas, in other situations the curriculum developer must identify the need.

Once a training need has been identified, a job analysis is conducted. The job analysis is done to provide a detailed list of the job steps that must be completed in the course of a job effort.

A task analysis is completed next. The task analysis provides a detailed breakdown of the job tasks into specific steps or segments. Next, trainee skills are assessed or estimated to determine their level of knowledge and skill for each of the stated tasks.

The results of the needs identification and analysis process is an indication of what needs to be taught. This list of needed training becomes a direct input to the development of training objectives, which is covered in the following chapter.

Additional References

Finch, Curtis R., & Cunkilton, John R. (1984)
Curriculum Development in Vocational and Technical Education: Planning, Content, and Implementation.
London : Allyn and Bacon, Inc.

Miller, Wilbur R. (1990)
Instructors and Their Jobs.
Illinois : American Technical Publishers, Inc.

Nadler, Leonard. (1982)
Designing Training Programmes:
The Critical Events Model.
Reading, Massachusetts : Addison-Wesley.

Posner, George J. and Rudnitsky, Alan N. (1986)
Course Design:
A Guide to Curriculum Development for Teachers.
White Plains, New York : Longman.

Wulf, Kathleen M., and Schave', Barbara. (1984)
Curriculum Design: A Handbook for Educators.
London : Scott, Foresman and Company.

Specify training objectives

CHAPTER 4

4

Specialty training objectives

CHAPTER 4 / SPECIFY TRAINING OBJECTIVES

Overview

Training involves meeting the instructional needs of people. Training which fails to meet learning needs is a waste of time, effort, and resources. In the previous chapter, you learned that needs assessment, or determining training needs, is the basis for all instruction. If there is a deficiency in peoples' performance that can be attributed to a lack of knowledge or skill then there is a training need. Once it has been determined that there is a need worth meeting, you have to describe that need as an objective to be realised. After completing your needs assessment, you are fairly confident of your focus and you know what must be taught. The next step is to state exactly what you want the trainees to accomplish and also what you are willing to accept as proof that they have met these goals.

Training objectives are the foundation of effective training. Unless training objectives are developed, a lesson cannot be systematically designed to achieve particular outcomes. Trainees expect their training to be useful to them. When you develop appropriate training objectives, you are taking the first step in ensuring that the training meets your trainees' needs.

This chapter covers the development of objectives for training. After carefully reading and studying this chapter you should be able to identify and develop appropriate learning objectives that describe to your trainees what they will know or be able to do as a result of your training.

The Role of Objectives

Instructional goals are fairly broad statements which describe general intended outcomes of training programmes. For example, a statement which claims "trainees will be better able to manage the records of their business" is an appropriate description of a general outcome expected from a training programme designed to teach trainees how to manage business records. It helps to define the general direction in which the programme is headed. However, the statement does not define exactly what the trainees will be

PREPARING TRAINING OBJECTIVES

SECTION II / DEVELOPING CURRICULUM

able to do in order to better manage the records of their business.

Instruction is successful, or effective, to the degree that it accomplishes what it sets out to accomplish. The changes you set out to accomplish through your training are your objectives. Objectives are statements of what a trainee will be able to do at the end of a training session. The reason for setting learning objectives is to ensure that both the trainer and the trainees know what target or outcome is being sought through the training activity. As the trainer, you must know exactly where you are going, otherwise you may get lost enroute. Trainees must know where they are going, otherwise they will not know what is expected of them.

Without measurable training objectives, learning cannot be successfully planned or evaluated. Learning objectives focus both the trainer and the trainee on the achievement of specific results.

❶ Objectives help the trainer develop and conduct training that provides the trainees with the knowledge and skills they need.

❷ Objectives provide the trainees with a clear understanding of what they will be expected to do as a result of the training.

❸ Objectives help both the trainer and the trainee evaluate the learning that has taken place through instruction.

Your training objectives should be developed to serve as a guide to learning, a guide to instruction, and a guide to evaluation.

Preparing Training Objectives

In many of the writings on objectives you will often find the term "performance" or "behavioural" objective used. This means that objectives are stated as behaviours that can be

PREPARING TRAINING OBJECTIVES

CHAPTER 4 / SPECIFY TRAINING OBJECTIVES

observed in a trainee. As a trainer you want to be able to determine your success or failure at the end of a training activity. It is therefore necessary that you be able to "observe" or "measure" changes in knowledge, skills, or attitudes among trainees. A performance or behavioural objective is an objective stated in a way that tells you and the trainees exactly what performance you want to be able to observe or measure at the end of training.

It is important that the training objectives for your training activities be realistic. They should come as close as possible to the actual behaviour the trainees will be expected to perform when on the job and should be viewed by trainees as both worthwhile and attainable.

A performance objective contains three pieces of information:

❶ **Conditions**, which describe the situation, limits, supplies, materials, tools, and equipment under which the behaviour will be performed

❷ **Performance**, which states what observable behaviour the trainee must demonstrate; and

❸ **Standards**, which describe how much is required or how precisely the quality of work must be performed.

CONDITIONS

You should describe the conditions under which trainee performance is to be observed. The circumstances or restrictions imposed on the trainee when he or she is demonstrating the behaviour should be defined. Frequently, the conditions of a performance objective identify the testing situation used to determine student achievement of the objective. For example, can trainees use their own tools? Is there a time limitation? Can they ask for help? Conditions can be best expressed with phrases such as "without reference to a manual" or "on your own".

Other examples of conditions are:

- Given a list of examples. . . . .
- Given a list of terms. . . . .
- While in the laboratory. . . . .
- Using a soil sampling kit. . . . .
- After observing a videotape. . . . .

PERFORMANCE

The most important characteristic of an objective is that it identifies the kind of behaviour or performance that will be required as evidence that a trainee has achieved the intended outcome. In a performance objective you should describe the trainee's expected behaviour as a precise, observable, and measurable outcome. You should describe what a trainee is expected to do upon completion of training. It can involve knowledge, skill, or attitude. You should use performance verbs which denote observable behaviour such as "define," "diagram," and "collect" in describing expected behaviour or performance. Performance verbs are much more effective than "fuzzy" verbs such as "know," "understand," or "learn." Performance verbs are more directly observable. For example, "the trainee will describe" is more exact than "the trainee will learn" and, thus, more useful in describing behaviour. Examples of other inappropriate words that do not describe specific observable behaviour are: appreciate, value, be aware of, remember, grasp, and believe. (Lists of suggested performance verbs to describe behaviour are provided in this chapter.)

Examples of performance statements are:

- The trainee will define in writing. . . . .
- The trainee will identify the components. . . . .
- The trainee will collect a soil sample. . . . .
- The trainee will lubricate all critical points. . . . .
- The trainee will determine the kind of nutrients. . . . .

PREPARING TRAINING OBJECTIVES

CHAPTER 4 / SPECIFY TRAINING OBJECTIVES

STANDARDS

Trainees may fail because they did not know how well you expected them to perform. The performance standard communicates to the trainee the quantity and quality of how well you expect the task to be completed. You should describe how well the trainee must perform in order to be considered acceptable. Standards answer such questions as "How often?" "How well?" "How many?" "How fast?" "In what sequence?" or "According to what standard procedures?" The standard can be stated in terms such as actual percentage of achievement, accuracy expected, number of errors permitted, time allowed to complete the task, or any other appropriate level at which achievement is anticipated. You should write standards in quantitative terms whenever possible. When this is not possible, you should try to use the most specific verbal terms possible; for example, "until the mixture is completely smooth."

Examples of performance standards are:

- . . . . . accurate to the nearest tenth.
- . . . . . according to the steps listed in the manual.
- . . . . . within twenty minutes.
- . . . . . at a rate of 100 per hour.
- . . . . . without any errors.

The following format, or some paraphrase of it, should be adequate for almost every training objective you write, no matter what the area of learning:

Sample format for a Training Objective

GIVEN (Here you state the condition)

THE TRAINEE WILL (Here you state the performance and the standard)

Here is an example. Suppose that while conducting your needs assessment you learned that agronomists were quite often required to collect soil samples, but that most of them were performing this task incorrectly. You therefore decided that one of your training activities should cover this topic. A performance objective for the training activity might look like this:

Sample Objective

Given *a soil sampling kit and a field plot* the trainee will *collect a representative soil sample and correctly label it for laboratory analysis.*

Categories of Performance Objectives

There are three main types of observable behaviour exhibited by trainees. As a trainer you can observe and evaluate the trainees':

❶ Knowledge and intellectual abilities

❷ Physical action and motor skills

❸ Feelings and attitudes

These categories will now be described and sample objectives presented. For each category a list of performance verbs is provided which you should find helpful when writing your objectives. Often the same performance verb will appear in two different categories. Depending on the context in which it is used, the same verb can describe behaviour in two different categories. Of course the lists are only guides. After a little practice, you will find other verbs to be more descriptive of expected behaviour in some of your training activities.

Knowledge and intellectual abilities range from simple recall of factual information through complex mental

CATEGORIES OF PERFORMANCE OBJECTIVES

CHAPTER 4 / SPECIFY TRAINING OBJECTIVES

processes. The following are examples of performance verbs used for writing objectives in the knowledge and intellectual abilities category.

Verbs for knowledge and intellectual abilities		
apply	diagnose	justify
assign	differentiate	label
average	discriminate	list
classify	discuss	name
compare	distinguish	prepare
conclude	estimate	qualify
contrast	evaluate	rate
decide	examine	recall
define	explain	repeat
demarcate	identify	select
demonstrate	illustrate	state
design	interpret	summarise
devise		

The following are examples of performance objectives in the knowledge and intellectual abilities category:

Example: *Given a geographical area, the trainee will identify the one crop that is most likely to provide the greatest yield.*

Example: *Given a list of generic drugs, the trainee will identify the antibiotics with 95% accuracy.*

Example: *Upon completion of the assigned reading and classroom training, the trainee will correctly identify types of soils by their characteristics.*

Example: *After completing the assigned training, the trainee will identify and define fifteen terms integral to understanding and using pesticides.*

73

CATEGORIES OF PERFORMANCE OBJECTIVES

SECTION II / DEVELOPING CURRICULUM

Example: Following a presentation and discussion of the topic, the trainee will correctly describe the basic principles of genetics and reproduction.

Example: Given a mixture of soybean meal and corn, use the square method to determine the proper proportion of each within 0.5 parts needed to provide a certain percentage of crude protein.

Physical action and motor skills includes competencies in the physical performance of an occupational skill or task. The following are examples of performance verbs used for writing objectives in the physical action and motor skills category.

Verbs for physical action and motor skills

adjust	collect	dip
administer	collimate	dismantle
agitate	connect	dispose
approach	construct	dissect
assemble	control	distinguish
bandage	cook	drain
bend	cool	draw
blend	coordinate	dry
boil	cover	duplicate
brew	cut	fasten
build	debark	feed
burn	debeak	fill
bury	define	filter
can	defoliate	fit
castrate	dehorn	fix
calibrate	dehydrate	formulate
centre	demonstrate	fumigate
change	develop	germinate
clean	dilute	grease
		(continues)

CATEGORIES OF PERFORMANCE OBJECTIVES

Verbs for physical action and motor skills

guide	position	stretch
handle	pump	strike
hang	pour	switch
harrow	prepare	tally
harvest	prune	taste
heat	puncture	thresh
impound	process	tighten
irrigate	produce	till
knead	raise	tilt
lacerate	record	touch
lubricate	reduce	tranfer
maintain	remove	transplant
mash	repair	transport
measure	report	trim
milk	reset	turn
mince	revise	twist
mix	revive	type
moisten	shear	use
mold	spray	vaccinate
move	sprinkle	wash
mulch	stain	wean
operate	start	weigh
perform	stock	winnow
pin	stop	wipe
place	store	wrap
plant	straighten	write
plough	streak	

The following are examples of performance objectives in the physical action and motor skills category:

Example: *Given an animal and the necessary equipment, the trainee will prepare a blood sample according to the specifications outlined in the handout provided.*

Example: *Given two objects, the trainee will weigh each object within 0.5 gram of their correct weight.*

Example: *Given the proper equipment, the trainee will sharpen agricultural tools using the steps outlined in class.*

Example: *Given the necessary equipment, the trainee will perform dehorning, castrating, and docking of animals according to the steps listed in the manual.*

Example: *Given necessary materials, the trainee will collect a water sample according to the steps outlined by the trainer.*

Feelings and attitudes are observable emotions or indications of acceptance or rejection. The following are examples of performance verbs used for writing objectives in the feelings and attitudes category.

CATEGORIES OF PERFORMANCE OBJECTIVES

CHAPTER 4 / SPECIFY TRAINING OBJECTIVES

Verbs for feelings and attitudes

accept	develop	prefer
acclaim	devote	promote
adhere	differentiate	propose
advocate	discuss	protest
agree	discriminate	pursue
applaud	display	question
approve	dispute	read
argue	evaluate	realise
ask	examine	receive
assist	favour	recommend
attempt	follow	reject
attend	formulate	relinquish
augment	give	request
avoid	help	resist
balance	influence	resolve
believe	invite	respond
challenge	investigate	revise
change	initiate	seek
choose	join	select
combine	judge	share
commend	justify	specify
compare	listen	subscribe
complete	modify	suggest
comply	obey	support
conform	object	test
control	observe	theorise
cooperate	organise	try
criticise	participate	verify
debate	persist	visit
decide	practice	volunteer
defend	praise	weigh

The following are examples of performance objectives in the feelings and attitudes category:

Example: *In the training setting, the trainee will assume responsibility for arriving on time every day within 2 minutes of the hour.*

Example: *Given a choice of several ways to apply pesticides, the trainee will choose to use the safest method.*

Example: *Presented with a new way to control pests, the trainee will accept the change and promote it to others.*

Example: *After proper demonstration and supervised practice, the trainee will decide to use tools in a safe way.*

Figure 4.1 shows additional examples of performance objectives that have been divided into the three components - conditions, performance and standard.

CATEGORIES OF
PERFORMANCE OBJECTIVES

CHAPTER 4 / SPECIFY TRAINING OBJECTIVES

Fig. 4.1 — EXAMPLES OF KNOWLEDGE, SKILLS AND ATTITUDE OBJECTIVES

Conditions	Performance	Standards
KNOWLEDGE-BASE		
❶ Referring to the list of names of plant diseases	the trainee will be able to classify the diseases	into pathological and non-pathological
❷ Based on the list of cost-benefit s potential of various crops	the trainee will justify	the one crop that is most beneficial
KNOWLEDGE AND SKILL-BASE		
❶ Provided with several multi-media extension materials	the trainee will select and present	the appropriate materials for group training
❷ Given a number of classroom training equipment	the trainee will demonstrate the operation	of at least three equipment
ATTITUDE-BASE		
❶ After participating in method and result demonstrations	the trainee will agree to	the recommended procedure
❷ After reviewing various options to utilise irrigation water	the trainee will comply with	the irrigation method that optimises water resources utilisation

SUMMARY

SECTION II / DEVELOPING CURRICULUM

Checklist for Writing Performance Objectives

❶ Remember that objectives refer to what the trainee is expected to do and not to what you are going to do. Objectives describe trainee behaviour not trainer duties or the learning process. Check your objectives to make sure they describe what trainees will be able to do when they have mastered the skill.

❷ Write objectives in simple, straightforward language. Objectives which are too long, use unnecessarily big words, or try to cover too many expected behaviours confuse trainees   Check to make sure your objectives communicate well and cover one learning outcome rather than several.

❸ Make sure your objectives identify expected trainee performance in clear terms. Check to be sure the performance verbs are not ambiguous or the content badly defined.

❹ Do not use too many objectives. You should have as few objectives as possible, and they should serve as clear guidelines for your training.

❺ Review your objectives to make sure they include the performance and the conditions and standards for performance. Check to be sure that the performance is observable and measurable and that it is a specific rather than a general performance.

❻ Make sure your objectives describe relevant behaviour and that they are attainable. You need to make sure your objectives are viewed by trainees as worthwhile and as possible to achieve.

Summary   Identifying and developing performance objectives is a key step in the curriculum development process. Objectives serve as important guidelines for developing the instruction, communicating expectations to trainees, and for designing measures of trainee performance. Objectives focus your attention and the trainees' attention on the achievement of results.

This chapter has presented a three-component guide to the writing of performance objectives. The three components are condition, performance, and standard. Sample performance objectives included in the chapter show how these three components can be used to make effective, clear statements of objectives for different training activities. The examples also illustrate that performance objectives can be written for training activities that focus on knowledge, skill, and attitude gains.

Additional References

Davies, Ivor K. (1981)
Instructional Technique.
New York, New York : McGraw-Hill, Inc.

Gagne, Robert .M., Briggs, Leslie.J.
and Wagner, Walter W. (1988)
Principles of Instructional Design.
New York, New York : Holt, Rinehart and Winston, Inc.

Hemp, Paul E. (1974)
How to Write and Use Behavioral Objectives in Vocational Education Programmes.
Danville, Illinois : The Interstate Printers & Publishers.

Mager, Robert F. (1975)
Preparing Instructional Objectives.
Belmont, California : Fearon Publishers, Inc.

CHAPTER 5

Identify and organise training content

PRINCIPLES OF LEARNING

CHAPTER 5 / IDENTIFY AND ORGANISE TRAINING CONTENT

Overview

The process of identifying content has already been initiated if you have conducted a job analysis, a task analysis and have written training objectives. These activities are all aimed at determining what to teach in a training course or programme. This chapter provides you with suggestions on how to interpret objectives into topics of instruction. This is accomplished by analysing each objective in terms of its underlying knowledge, skill and attitude requirements.

Additionally, this chapter is focused on helping you decide how to organise and sequence content. The sequencing of content is very important because it may have a significant effect on the amount and efficiency of learning. You would not think of teaching someone how to select insecticides before he or she knows something about insect identification. If you choose the wrong order of content, both you and the trainees will be confused and frustrated.

Another important aspect of this chapter involves suggestions on how to record your curriculum and scheme for instruction into a course plan. The lesson plan typically includes a course description, a syllabus, and a series of lesson plans. This aspect of the chapter will be built upon in the two following chapters that deal with selecting training methods and determining needed resources.

Principles of Learning

Training involves the facilitation of learning by individuals or groups of people who can benefit by having new knowledge, skills or attitudes. Consequently, it is useful to understand some of the underlying principles of learning. These principles should be considered as one designs a curriculum and delivers instruction.

Trainers, especially new trainers or trainers who have not been professionally prepared in training methodology, enter the training situation with an image of training that resembles how they were taught in primary school, secondary school or the university. Most of this image is based on experience as a young person. However, in extension and agricultural training we are usually dealing with adult men and women. There are distinct differences in the way that people learn in formal and nonformal education. Table 5.1 presents some of the differences that exist between the two learning contexts

TABLE 5.1 SEVERAL LEARNING DIFFERENCES BETWEEN NONFORMAL AND FORMAL EDUCATION

Nonformal/Adult Education	Formal Education
Learners:	**Learners:**
Decide for themselves what is important to be learned	Rely on others to decide what is important to learn
Need to validate the information against their beliefs and experience	Generally accept the information being taught without question
Are experienced and may have fixed views	Have little or no experience from which to draw and more open to information
May have extensive knowledge and able to provide information and assistance to other trainees	Have little ability to help others with the content of instruction
Expect what they are learning to be immediately useful	Expect to use the new knowledge and skills sometime in the future

The differences identified in the table reveal the need to focus the training on the specific trainees and to recognise that nonformal education, often referred to as training, in the agriculture setting may be much different from formal education in the common school.

A very important step in planning for training is knowing the trainees. *Chapter 3* suggested that you assess the current level of proficiency of trainees. This process should not stop there. As a trainer, you must constantly be assessing the current level of learning of trainees. The first session of training can be used to reveal trainee proficiency. Having trainees talk about their experience, providing opportunity for questions from trainees and posing direct and probing questions to trainees can all help you to understand better the proficiency and needs of trainees.

A good trainer is able to assess proficiency and needs throughout the course of instruction and continuously adjust training to these needs. This means that a certain amount of flexibility must be built into the curriculum. If too rigid, the trainer may fail to take advantage of the experience that exists within the group or to meet new needs that arise.

There are a number of general learning principles that should be considered as one designs a curriculum. These principles also become important as instruction is delivered.

LEARNING PRINCIPLE 1.

The trainee must be motivated to learn

Since motivation is an individual and unique function, the trainer must be deliberate and creative about identifying motivators for the group being served. These motivators can be presented in the overview of the course to trainees, at the beginning of each lesson, and built into the instruction itself.

LEARNING PRINCIPLE 2.

Learning is an active and participatory process

This means that the trainees must be involved in the learning and not just be listening to the trainer. Involvement can occur in many forms: through questioning, discussion, practice sessions, field work, role playing, demonstrations by trainees, and so on. The curriculum or lesson plan must incorporate activities to ensure this principle is included.

LEARNING PRINCIPLE 3.

The trainee must have guidance and feedback

Training must include providing feedback to trainees so that they know how well they are learning and so they know when they have mastered a skill. Trial and error is not an efficient nor motivating method for learning most things. Instead, the trainer must provide guidance and feedback.

LEARNING PRINCIPLE 4.

Appropriate training materials must be provided

Materials that support training must be effectively prepared and used. Case problems, projects, practice activities, discussions, and many other methods must include useful and explanatory materials to ensure and support learning.

LEARNING PRINCIPLE 5.

The opportunity to practise must be built into training

Experience and research have shown that practice of new knowledge and skills assists in their retention. Trainers must be cautious to provide the time and structure for practice. Practice can help in building confidence as well as providing the opportunity for trainees to help each other learn.

LEARNING PRINCIPLE 6.

Training methods should be varied

As you will read in the next chapter, training methods should be selected to match the particular type of learning and the training setting. Additionally, you will realise that more than one method will usually suffice for the same training task. Consequently, when possible, the trainer should use multiple methods and techniques. This will stimulate the trainees' interest and provide variety for all involved.

LEARNING PRINCIPLE 7.

Trainees must receive

Trainees must know when they have performed a task or learned subject matter correctly. They must receive some indication of this. This reinforcement can take the form of a positive comment from the trainer, the grade on an examination, or the successful operation of a product or

reinforcement of desired behaviour

project used in training. In any case, reinforcement must be planned for and incorporated in the lesson plan.

LEARNING PRINCIPLE 8.

Standards of performance and expectations should be clearly communicated to trainees

The use of training objectives with their three necessary components, as described in *Chapter 4*, provide an excellent means for accommodating this principle.

LEARNING PRINCIPLE 9.

There exist different kinds and levels of learning

Learning can be classified into three major categories as described in *Chapter 4*. These include: 1) Knowledge and intellectual abilities, 2) Physical action and motor skills, and 3) Feelings and attitudes. Each of these categories has levels within them. For example in knowledge and intellectual abilities the levels range from remembering facts to analysing complex structures and concepts. These different types and levels of learning may require different methods and different practice opportunities. These must be planned into the training.

These general principles related to learning are important to training design or curriculum development. When developing a new training programme or designing a training lesson, you should review these principles so that they are in mind as you plan.

In agricultural training, skill acquisition usually becomes the main objective. Trainees need to acquire some skills in performing their work. While the above learning principles can serve as a guide, trainers should, if possible, use field-based training to allow trainees to practice the skills.

Principles for Organising Content

The sequencing of training content is an important step in the curriculum development process. If training content is derived from job and task analysis as suggested in *Chapter 3*, it is obvious that a job and its tasks have a logical and sometimes necessary sequence. Additionally, there is a necessary and efficient sequence for learning. This section provides four general principles for organising content that will make training more effective and more efficient.

ORGANISING PRINCIPLE 1.

Move from simple to complex

People can relate to small, simple events, tasks or facts more easily than they can to complex ones. Also, by beginning with simple items and progressing to more complex ones, you can reinforce the learning of simple items progressively, thus increasing confidence of the trainee. Since complex concepts and equipment are made up of simpler parts, it is logical to present and teach the parts before teaching the whole. For example, you would teach the farmer the main parts of a tank sprayer before you would teach him or her the use of the sprayer. Understanding and recognising the parts makes it much more effective to teach its use.

ORGANISING PRINCIPLE 2.

Move from general to specifics

Oftentimes people are more familiar with generalised concepts than with specifics. This is true especially when the generalised concepts can be easily understood. In teaching, it gives trainees a clearer picture if you start with the general concept before proceeding to specifics. For example, if you are teaching a group of trainees on pest control, you would start by talking about crop damage caused by pests. However, as you progress from there, you discuss the types of crop damage caused by insect pests and diseases and their control. As you get familiar with the concept, you introduce more specifics like the type and number of insect pests and pathogens present in the crop that caused the damage and types of control methods.

ORGANISING PRINCIPLE 3.

Use an existing logical organisation

There is an inherent logic or normal system of organisation to some content. For example, if one is training extension workers in proper crop storage procedures, there may be a natural sequence in which crops are harvested. Consequently, you might organise the training according to which crop is harvested first in the year, then move to the next crop in the sequence. This is called a chronological sequence. Another type of logical sequence is topical. For example, you might teach farmers about the characteristics of all relevant fertilisers for their situation before you would instruct them on application of each. Another form of organisation is learning ease. Some trainees may prefer to learn things in a particular sequence because of their past learning experience, their cultural values, or simply their preference. You should be sensitive to these needs and organise content accordingly.

ORGANISING PRINCIPLE 4.

Move from known to unknown

Learning theory tells us that people build their knowledge and skills by adding and connecting to what they already know or can do. Therefore, as a trainer and curriculum developer, you should structure and sequence content so that it begins with current knowledge of the trainees and moves to new knowledge. Also, one can take known concepts and adapt them or relate them to new, similar concepts. The use of analogies is an example of moving from known to unknown.

ORGANISING PRINCIPLE 5.

Use job performance order

Job performance order involves organising the training according to the natural order that tasks are completed on the job. For example, if training is focused on the disassembly of a water pump for irrigation, the training might occur in the order of the steps used to disassemble the pump. This makes the training extremely relevant and easy for the trainees to observe.

Course Planning

Planning for training represents the broadest level for identifying and organising content. A course is a major segment of training that is focused on a single major topic. A one week training activity for farmers, a two month programme for extension experts, or a three month session for subject matter specialists, are examples of training courses. A course is made up of units or lessons. Content identification and organisation for lessons are covered in the next section.

Course planning involves the development of two separate but related documents. These documents are: the **Course Description** and the **Lesson Plans** which comprise the curriculum. The course description or syllabus provides an overview of the course and is designed to inform trainees and potential trainees about the course. The curriculum outlines the entire training course and it provides a specific guide to the trainer. The specific guide includes a content outline for each major topic (lesson plans), the methods that will be used, the time estimate for each major topic, needed resources, and other pertinent information.

Course Description

The course description is a simple overview of the training course. It has a number of uses. It can be used to inform potential training participants, to inform policy makers or supervisors, and it can be used to introduce trainees to the course. Essentially, it is an introduction to the course.

The course description typically includes the following sections:

❶ Course Title,

❷ Purpose of the Course,

❸ Course Objectives,

❹ Training Methods and Techniques,

❺ Intended Audience of the Course,

❻ Venue of Training,

❼ Logistical Arrangements,

❽ Duration and Schedule of the Course, and

❾ Trainers/Resource Persons.

Course Title

The course title should reflect the purpose and content of the course. It should be as specific as possible and should indicate content covered, type of training and level of training. The following examples provide ideas for course titles.

> **Sample Course Titles**
>
> ■ Basic Principles Of Tillage: Skills For Grain Farmers.
> ■ Practical Application Of Fertilisers For Farmers.
> ■ Sprayer Use For Pesticides In Rice Production.
> ■ Rodent Control In Rice Fields For Vietnamese Farmers.

A good check on the appropriateness of a title is to ask the question, "If I read this title would I know what the course is about and for whom it is designed?

Purpose of the Course

This section should include one or two paragraphs that describe the general rationale for the course. This should include a statement regarding the reason this course

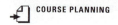
COURSE PLANNING

SECTION II / DEVELOPING CURRICULUM

has been designed and is being offered. A list of benefits that should accrue from the course may also be included in this section.

Sample Purpose of the Course

This course is designed to assist rice farmers in Vietnam to better control rodents in their rice fields. The course has come about from two major studies that have been done in the country related to the productivity of rice growers. These studies have revealed that rodents are a major cause of crop loss. A series of preventive and corrective techniques have been included in this course. If course participants use these techniques, it is expected that their rice production can increase up to 30 percent.

Course Objectives

It is here that you include a list of the course objectives in a format similar to that suggested in *Chapter 4*. These general objectives will provide the reader of the course description with a deeper understanding of the purpose and intent of the course. Additionally, it will provide an overview of the content of the course.

As the course objectives are listed, attention should be paid to their sequence. As suggested earlier in this chapter, you should use one or more of the organising principles in sequencing the objectives. Essentially, what you are doing at this stage is determining the general outline of the course. The development of the lesson plan in the next section of this chapter will require you to expand on each objective in terms of content. The following course objectives are examples:

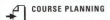

CHAPTER 5 / IDENTIFY AND ORGANISE TRAINING CONTENT

Sample Course Objectives

❶ To introduce to the trainees the major rodents present in the rice fields of Vietnam.

❷ To enable the trainees to determine rice plant damages caused by pests.

❸ To help trainees determine the major cause of rice plant damage by rodents.

❹ To introduce to trainees the appropriate corrective and preventive rodent control techniques.

Training Methods and Techniques

This section deals with how trainers conduct training activities to achieve the course objectives. The most appropriate training method is selected based on the training objectives, type of trainees and the training environment. Thus, trainers select the training method that best fits the course content and desired outcome. There are various methods/approaches in training that are commonly used such as lectures, group discussions, demonstrations, field/practical exercises, role play, case studies and field visits.

Sample Training Methods

The course will utilise the following training methods:

❶ Classroom lectures.

❷ Group work, discussion and critique sessions.

❸ Field visits.

❹ Assigned reading.

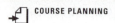

SECTION II / DEVELOPING CURRICULUM

Intended Audience of the Course

This brief section identifies whom the course has been designed for and who should be recruited and enrolled in the course. This section may change as the course is moved from one area, country or region to another. The reader of the course description should know exactly who is or should be in the course. The following example states who should be involved.

Sample Intended Audience Statement

This course is intended for rice farmers in the northern part of Vietnam. Any farmer who is responsible for one hectare or more should plan to attend this course. The government will pay the cost of the course, and the participant is responsible for transportation to and from the course.

Venue of the Training

This section should adequately describe the place where the course will be offered. It should provide enough detail so that a potential participant can locate the place of the course. The following is an example venue statement.

Sample Venue Statement

This course will be held at the extension training centre of Nam Pen located on the road to Ho Chi Minh City north of Lon Tu.

CHAPTER 5 / IDENTIFY AND ORGANISE TRAINING CONTENT

Logistical Arrangements

This section provides information or a guide to trainees on the types of facilities available, such as accommodation, transport, course materials, and meals during the course. Information on training expenses and cost should also be specified. It is important to describe these facilities so that trainees can prepare or make the necessary arrangements before attending the course. The following is a sample logistical arrangements:

Sample Logistical Arrangements

Meals and accommodation will be at the Centre's dormitary. Total cost of meals and accommodation is US$350.00 per participant. Participants' travel expenses from their districts to Ho Chi Minh City to be borne by the Rice IPM Network.

Duration and Schedule of the Course

This section should communicate when the course will be offered and the length of time required to complete it. This statement should include the dates the course will begin and end, the time of day instruction begins and the time of day the course will end. This information will be crucial to the scheduling of transportation and lodging so that training is not hampered by late arrival. A sample course duration and schedule is as follows:

Sample Duration and Schedule

The 3-day course will begin on 5 December 1994 at 9:00 a. m. and will end on 7 December 1994 at 5:00 p.m.

LESSON PLANS

Trainers/Resource Persons

This section should indicate who will be responsible for providing the training. This will provide the participants with an indication of whom they will be dealing with, and if necessary, whom they must communicate with in advance of the training. A sample list of trainer/resource person is as follows:

Sample List of Trainer/Resource Person

1. **Kim Wey Siu**
   Regional Extension Specialist,
   Ho Chi Minh City, Vietnam
2. **Nguyen Van Thien**
   Rodent Specialist,
   Plant Protection Department,
   Ho Chi Minh City, Vietnam

Each of the sections described for the course description helps to provide an overview of the course to those who may be interested. Two examples of course description are presented in Section III. The distribution and use of the course description will vary depending on need and purpose. For example, it might be posted to farmers, handed to farmers at a community meeting, published in a newspaper, or handed out to course participants at the beginning of a course.

Lesson Plans

The lesson plan is the blueprint and guide for conducting training activities. It tells the trainer what to do and when. The lesson plan is designed for specific use by the trainer. However, a lesson plan can be developed in various formats. In this *Guide*, two examples are illustrated in Section III. The plan is usually designed by the trainer as he or she is developing the course. It may also be used by another trainer who assists in teaching the course or another trainer who might teach the course in a different location to a different group of participants. The plan incorporates the following segments or components:

① Objectives,

② Content Outline,

③ Training Methods,

④ Time Estimates,

⑤ Needed Training Resources,

⑥ Participant Assignments, and

⑦ Evaluation Method.

When the lesson plan is complete it provides a logical organisation for the course. The completion of each of the segments of the plan provides a record of the entire curriculum. Therefore, the lesson plan represents the body of the curriculum. The curriculum consists of the course description and all the lesson plans.

The lesson plan, in addition to documenting the curriculum, provides a guide to the trainer as he or she prepares to teach the course and as he or she presents the course. The lesson plan, even though prepared in advance of training, must also be flexible. If certain learning difficulties are encountered, if new ideas and topics are revealed during instruction, or if participant needs are clarified, the lesson plan can be adjusted accordingly. Also, if the course is taught more than once, the plan can be revised for the second offering to reflect what was learned in the first course offering. The following sections provide a brief description of each of the suggested elements of the lesson plan.

Objectives

As explained earlier, the lesson plan can be divided into segments or components. Each of these should be sequenced according to one or more of the organising principles cited in the previous section of this chapter. The segments can be designed to parallel the course objectives or subdivision of the objectives. Training objectives at the lesson plan level should be more specific and contain the three parts of an objective's statement: the conditions, performance and standards. Such an objective statement will enable the trainer to plan his training activities within the time of the lesson. In addition it also enables the trainer to observe and the measure trainee's performance. Thus the trainer will be able to evaluate the effectiveness of the training. The following is a sample of a training objective:

Sample Training Objective

Rodent Control in Rice Fields for Vietnamese Farmers

Objective: On completion of the lesson, the trainees will be able to identify four major rodents present in the rice fields of Vietnam.

Content Outline

This section of the lesson plan is the most significant one and usually takes the greatest amount of space. The content outline must contain the information that will be taught during the training. The content should be derived directly from the objectives. The following steps provide a suggested procedure for deriving the topics and subtopics to be included in training.

STEP 1.

Identify the knowledge that is necessary to accomplish the objective

This is accomplished by analysing the objective. This involves dissecting the objective into its parts. Knowledge includes facts, concepts and principles that must be remembered or understood in order to accomplish the objective. If you are a content expert, you can determine the knowledge requirements of the objective from your own knowledge and experience. If you are not an expert, then you must read technical documents, consult with subject matter experts or talk with people who routinely accomplish the objective in the course of their work. It should be obvious that much of this analysis information can be gleaned from the job and task analysis that you completed earlier.

In the following *Sample Objective 1* statement, there are three knowledge elements.

Sample Objective 1: On completion of the lesson, the trainees will be able to identify four major rodents present in the rice fields of Vietnam.

Knowledge elements

- Know definition of rodent
- List rodents of rice in Vietnam
- Recognise the damage of rodents to rice plants

These elements provide the knowledge content for training.

STEP 2.

Identify the performance or skill requirements of each objective

This step is accomplished in the same manner as the knowledge component identification. The difference is that one must look for required actions for accomplishment of the objectives. The question "What must someone do in order to accomplish the objective?" must be answered to identify skill requirements.

It should be noted that not all objectives will have a skill component. For example, *Sample Objective 1* is strictly a

LESSON PLANS

knowledge objective. Therefore, it has no skill requirements. However, many objectives have both knowledge and skill elements.

Sample Objective 2 below has both knowledge and skill elements. The knowledge elements are identified in Step 1. In this step you would list the skill requirements for this objective.

Sample Objective 2: on completion of this lesson, the trainees will be able to apply appropriate corrective and preventive rodent control measures.

Skill Elements

- Organise a group of field workers
- Select appropriate direction and location for attack
- Use appropriate tool or device for eradication
- Implement counting mechanism for eradication

STEP 3.

Identify important attitude elements for the objective

Many objectives have attitude elements, especially those that deal with crop and human safety. Someone can possess the necessary knowledge and skills, but without the proper attitude, may cause harm in accomplishing the objective. The following attitude element is important to *Sample Objective 2.*

Attitude Element

- Use proper safety practices
- Dispose of waste properly

STEP 4.

Organise the knowledge, skill and attitude (KSA's) elements into a logical sequence

The suggestions made earlier in this chapter should be considered. This organisation should be in the form of topics. Each topic can be subdivided where it seems appropriate to you as a trainer. The result is a topic outline for a training segment (a unit, lesson or part of a lesson). The subdivisions become subpoints in the outline.

STEP 5.

Record the topical outline onto the Lesson Plan Form

This can be done in differing degrees of detail. You should use the extent of detail that you are comfortable with. This outline will be your guide as you present the lesson to participants. New trainers usually include a great deal of detail in the content outline. This provides a support mechanism for instruction. More experienced trainers may use only the major topics in their outline because they may be more secure with the content and with training.

Training Methods

Once the content outline is prepared and recorded in the lesson plan, the appropriate methods should be selected and identified. The suggestions provided in *Chapter 6* should be consulted for this section. Variety and appropriateness should be kept in mind as your selection of methods is made.

Time Estimates

An estimate of the time needed for covering each major point or topic in the content outline should be made. This estimate will be based upon the amount of material that is subsumed by each topic and the method that has been selected. The time estimates will help ensure that the total course is completed and that some items are not over emphasised at the expense of others. These estimates are indicated in the training curricula examples in *Section III*.

Needed Training Resources

The training resources that are critical to the implementation of training and the accomplishment of the objectives should be carefully identified. These resources include the type of facility necessary, the type of equipment needed, and the instructional materials needed. By considering each topic in the content outline, and its relation to training method, an indication of needed resources can be derived.

Instructional materials such as overhead transparencies, activity sheets for demonstrations and practice exercises, photographs, slides, video tapes, workbooks and information handouts, are all examples of what might be used. It is important to identify these planning process so that they can be acquired or developed prior to the training taking place. *Chapter 7* provides suggestions for selecting and developing appropriate instructional materials. An example of information handout is provided in pages 249 - 253.

Participant Assignments

This section of the lesson plan should stipulate the activities and assignments that will be made to training participants as part of the training. Including these in the lesson plan facilitates the development of any needed materials for the assignments. Including the assignments in the lesson plan also serves as a reminder to give the assignments at the appropriate time during the training course.

Evaluation Method

The last section of the lesson plan should describe the technique, procedure and instrument for evaluating the accomplishment of course objectives by the participants, and the performance of resource persons for each session.

LESSON PLANS

CHAPTER 5 / IDENTIFY AND ORGANISE TRAINING CONTENT

These techniques might involve paper and pencil tests, performance tests, simulated work samples, or direct observation of performance. Each should be selected to match the objective being assessed. *Chapter 7* provides suggestions on selecting and developing appropriate evaluation instruments. An example of the evaluation form can be found on page 234.

Alternative Lesson Plan Formats

Lesson plans can take many different forms. Individual tainers should pick one or design one that fits their needs. The one on the following page is concise and provide only a general structure for the content of a lesson. The less experienced trainer may choose a much more detailed plan that contains detailed content outlines and presentation notes. *Section III* of this guide contains several different examples of lesson plan formats.

LESSON PLANS SECTION II / DEVELOPING CURRICULUM

BLANK LESSON PLAN FORM

LESSON PLAN

Course Title: ……………………………… Page …………….. of ……….

Lesson Title: ……………………………… Date ………………………………

Training Objectives:
On completion of this lesson, the trainees will be able to:
1.
2.
3.
4.

Topical Outline	Method	Time Estimate	Needed Resource

Practical/Field-Based Exercises:

Participant Assignment:

Evaluation Method:

LESSON PLANS

CHAPTER 5 / IDENTIFY AND ORGANISE TRAINING CONTENT

COMPLETED LESSON PLAN FORM

LESSON PLAN

Course Title: Rice Farming   **Page** .... **of** ....

Lesson Title: Fertilising   **Date** ....

Training Objectives:
On completion of this lesson, the trainees will be able to:
1. Collect soil samples for analysis.
2. Identify types of basal fertilisers for soil.
3. Determine amount of fertilisers required by soil.
4. Identify nutrient deficiency symptoms in plants.

Topical Outline	Method	Time Estimate	Needed Resource
Soil sample collection procedures	Demonstration	30 minutes	rice field shovel, container
Basal fertilisers found in soil	Discussion	30 minutes	fertiliser sample
Performing and interpreting soil analysis tests	Demonstration and practical	2 hours	soil sample test kits

Practical/Field-Based Exercises:
Go out to rice field, properly collect soil samples, inspect plants, and perform soil test procedures.

Participant Assignment:
Analyse soil and plant samples to determine nutrient deficiency symptoms.

Evaluation Method:
Comparison and review of student and instructor results.

Summary

Understanding the learning principles and how they apply specifically to adult trainees will guide the development of curriculum and will ensure a greater degree of success in the training effort. The organisation of course content is critical for the success of the programme. In the broadest sense such principles define a conceptual framework for organising and constructing the course.

Course planning consists of a series of focussing tasks and instruments designed to shape overall objectives into coherent and manageable units of instruction. Adhering to a disciplined and systematic approach from the beginning will enhance the training programme by providing a logical organisation of instructional units and a sense of continuity throughout the course.

Additional References

Finch, Curtis R., & Cunkilton, John R. (1984)
Curriculum Development in Vocational and Technical Education: Planning, Content, and Implementation.
London : Allyn and Bacon, Inc.

Miller, Wilbur R. (1990)
Instructors and Their Jobs.
Homewood, Illinois : American Technical Publishers, Inc.

Nadler, Leonard. (1982)
Designing Training Programmes:
The Critical Events Model.
Reading, Massachusetts : Addison-Wesley.

Posner, George J. and Rudnitsky, Alan N. (1986)
Course Design:
A Guide to Curriculum Development for Teachers.
White Plains, New York : Longman.

Wulf, Kathleen M., & Schave, Barbara. (1984)
Curriculum Design, A Handbook for Educators.
London : Scott, Foresman and Company.

Select training methods and techniques

CHAPTER 6

CHAPTER 6 / SELECT TRAINING METHODS AND TECHNIQUES

Overview

The previous chapters have helped you to focus your training by developing objectives and organising training content. As a trainer, you must also be concerned with providing trainees with learning activities that effectively present the content and help them accomplish training objectives.

A builder has many available tools from which to choose. The builder does not use the same tool for different tasks even though it might be a favourite tool. Each task is best accomplished by using the tool specifically designed for it. A hammer is good for driving nails but useless for digging holes. The trainer also has a number of teaching tools available which are particularly suited for producing a desired result.

This chapter covers selection of, and planning for, the general training approach and selection of training methods. Information is provided on the advantages and disadvantages of several training methods. Suggestions are given for selecting the most appropriate methods based on the training objectives, the types of trainees, and the training environment. After carefully reading and studying this chapter, you should be able to make good decisions about the general training approach to use. In addition, you should be able to select training methods that best fit the type of content and desired learning outcomes.

Determine The General Training Approach

Once it has been determined that training is needed, training objectives have been written, and the training content has been developed, the next step is to develop an overall strategy or approach for delivering the training. Determining the overall approach requires that you decide whether the training is to be delivered in a centralised or decentralised way, and whether it should be conducted in the classroom or in another setting. The duration of the training and the types of meetings must also be determined.

Centralisation Versus Decentralisation

One of the first questions to be answered is whether you will take the training to the trainees or they will be required to come to you. You need to weigh the benefits of having the trainees come to a centralised training location or facility versus taking the training to the field. Factors to consider include cost of travel, required facilities and equipment, number of trainees involved, speed of training delivery, whether the training is a one time activity or will be repeated often, and personal preferences of both trainers and trainees. Consideration of these factors should allow you to make a good decision about whether the training should be field based or centrally located.

Classroom Instruction

Perhaps as much as 95% of all formal adult training is conducted in classrooms. Advances such as computer-assisted instruction, closed-circuit television, teaching machines, and other developments have made progress toward bringing field conditions into the classroom. Classroom instruction remains extremely popular for several reasons. The ease of operation is probably the main reason for its popularity. It is fairly easy to do classroom instruction since all you have to do is find a room and assemble a group of trainees and an instructor. It may not be the best instruction, but it is relatively easy to initiate.

There are other reasons why the classroom is used so widely. In a classroom setting all trainees are given the same messages at the same time. Everyone starts and stops at the same time, and they all interact with the same people all the time. In other words, there is a great amount of control of the learning situation, both what is taught and how it is taught.

However, while the classroom setting is the most popular

among trainers, it is often not used effectively. It is just as easy to have bad training in the classroom as it is to have good training in the classroom. It may even be more likely to have bad training in the classroom. Some trainers think the only way to train is to tell trainees what they know. The traditional classroom setup often encourages this type of training. The classroom can provide a situation for getting people together who need to learn. They can be helped and stimulated by an effective trainer and can also learn from each other. It can bring together a variety of people with similar or different problems and allow them to interact and share solutions. If these outcomes are important to you, then classroom instruction is appropriate. However, if they are not, then you should also consider using some form of self- instruction by trainees.

Duration and Types of Classroom Meetings

Sometimes it is appropriate to schedule training on a regular and continuing basis; that is: several hours per week for an extended number of weeks. However, this model for scheduling training is rarely used outside the academic world. Instead, short-term, intensive meetings are conducted. These training sessions are often called seminars, conferences, or workshops.

A *seminar* is a meeting of individuals who come together to study a subject under the leadership of an expert. A specific problem is identified and discussed. The discussions and conclusions reached are usually based on research findings. An example seminar might be "New Developments in Chemical Weed Control."

Similarly, a *conference* is a meeting of a group of people representing different organisations who have some common interest or background. Like the seminar, the intent is to gather information and discuss mutual problems, with a reasonable solution as the desired end. The conference is often less specific and less focused on a single topic or problem. An example of a conference might be, "Weed Control in Rice in the Southeast Asia Region."

In a **workshop** a group of people with a common interest or problem, often related to their occupation, meet together for a period of time to improve their proficiency or understanding. Most of your training will be conducted in one of these settings.

Training is aimed at improving the skills or providing the knowledge needed to do particular jobs. Training programmes have very specific objectives that focus on one or more skills, areas of knowledge, or abilities. Therefore, the duration of training programmes varies widely. A training course may last several hours, one day, or several days. The length of training programmes should not depend on how much time is available. Rather you should plan the length of the training programme based on how long it will take to achieve the training objectives. Of course, how long it takes to meet training objectives depends on factors such as number of trainees involved, trainees' abilities, and complexity of the training content. However, length of training is also dependent upon the types of training methods you select.

Types Of Training Methods and Techniques

The use of a variety of training methods and techniques not only increases the interest of the trainees but also the programme effectiveness. It also encourages active participation by the audience. A training method is a strategy or tactic that you use to deliver the content so that the trainees will achieve the objectives. In using a specific training method, the trainer may also employ a variety of techniques to enhance the effectiveness of the learning process.

The selection and use of appropriate training methods and techniques in the training process serve two important purposes:

- They provide and ensure a means for the trainee to learn the specific training content you have identified.

- They help keep the trainee interested and involved in the training so that learning is enhanced.

There are a variety of training methods available to you as a trainer. The eight most commonly used methods are:

❶ Lecture/Instructor Presentation. You orally present new information to trainees using a variety of training techniques and communication tools.

❷ Group Discussion. You lead the group of trainees in discussing a topic. Group size may vary but discussion may be less effective if the group is too large.

❸ Demonstration. You show the correct steps for completing a task, or show an example of a correctly completed task. Various types of communication tools may be used during the demonstration.

❹ Reading. You give trainees written material to be read that presents new information.

❺ Exercises. You give trainees assignments to be completed related to the topic of the training activity.

❻ Case Study. You give trainees information about a situation and direct them to come a decision or solve a problem concerning the situation. It can be brief or lengthy.

❼ Role Play. Trainees act out a real life situation in an instructional setting.

❽ Field Visits/Study Tours. Trainees are given the opportunity to observe and interact with the problem being solved or skill being learned.

Additional information regarding each of these training methods, including a list of advantages and disadvantages of each, is provided for you on the following pages.

LECTURE/INSTRUCTOR PRESENTATION

A lecture or instructor presentation is the most common training/teaching method used, but it may not be the most effective. Instructor presentations are typically formal presentations of information by the trainer so that the trainees can listen, observe, and understand the concept, principle, or procedure being presented. It generally incorporates lecture technique with a variety of communication tools, such as printed materials, overhead transparencies, slides, video/film, specimens, exhibits, chalk and board, and computers. Instructor presentations have both advantages and disadvantages that you should consider.

Advantages of Lecture/Instructor Presentations

❶ You can keep the group together and focussed on the same point. You have complete control over both the content and the sequencing of the information.

❷ You can cover a large amount of material in a short time.

❸ You can easily control the schedule or time spent on topics.

❹ The instructor presentation is a familiar method to your trainees and they will probably be comfortable with it.

❺ You can use this method for large groups as long as you can be seen and heard.

❻ You can use instructor presentation when your physical facilities are limited.

LECTURE INSTRUCTOR PRESENTATION

Disadvantages of Lectur/Instructor Presentations

❶ You are likely to have only one-way communication.

❷ Your trainees are often passive learners.

❸ It is difficult to master effective lecturing.

❹ Your training can become dull if you use instructor presentation for too long without trainee participation.

❺ Instructor presentation can be inappropriate for learning practical subjects such as skill acquisition.

❻ It is difficult to gauge whether trainees are learning.

❼ Trainees do not remember as much as when they are actively involved in the learning process.

High quality, effective instructor presentations have several common characteristics regardless of the topic. Check to make sure your presentations have the following characteristics:

Characteristics of an Effective Instructor Presentation

❶ Purpose and objectives of the presentation are well understood by the trainees.

❷ The topic and language of your presentation are relevant to trainees' prior knowledge.

❸ The presentation is well organised to include an introduction and summary.

❹ The pace of your presentation is appropriate to the trainees.

❺ Trainees are in a comfortable environment, and your presentation can be seen and heard by all trainees.

❻ You are sensitive to the needs of trainees and adjust your presentation accordingly.

❼ You use questions frequently to check trainees' understanding.

Effective instructor presentations are usually supported with handouts, overhead transparencies, flip charts, slides, video/film, etc. Handouts are useful for providing facts and figures and can be used by trainees as follow-up materials to be reviewed later. You should make sure that your handouts are prepared at the reading level of the trainees in your class.

Overhead transparencies are portable, flexible, and can be useful in clarifying things that cannot be easily shown with real things. Your training location may restrict its use, since an overhead projector requires electricity.

Flip charts can serve as a guide and support for your presentations. They can be used effectively with large or small groups. They are inexpensive, flexible, reusable, and require no electricity or special equipment. However, flip charts are not good for presenting detailed information. They are time-consuming to use and are difficult to transport.

Slides, video or films are useful for illustrating complex activities that are not easily explained by other visuals.

GROUP DISCUSSION

A group discussion is a verbal exchange of ideas, points of view, subject matter, and perceptions among the trainer and the trainees for the purpose of clarifying or enriching understanding of the content you are covering in a training activity. Several techniques such as brainstorming and buzz sessions can be used to encourage participatory discussion. Group discussions have several advantages and disadvantages that you should consider.

Advantages of Group Discussions

❶ You can provide every trainee with the opportunity to participate, and therefore, keep them interested and involved.

❷ You can take advantage of the varied abilities, knowledge, and experiences of the entire class.

❸ If you properly plan and organise the group discussion, it can be highly stimulating and motivating for the trainees,

❹ You can observe how much learning is taking place.

Disadvantages of Group Discussions

❶ A group discussion can turn into an aimless debate unless you properly organise and control it.

❷ A few trainees may dominate the discussion.

❸ You can only use a group discussion effectively with a fairly small group of trainees. Seven can be considered optimal.

❹ Group discussions can take a lot of your training time and often important points can be confusing or lost.

Characteristics of an Effective Group Discussion

A group discussion can help you to stimulate or motivate trainees and is one way you can get trainees involved in the learning process. A group discussion also gives you a chance to develop cooperation among trainees and encourage sharing of ideas and different viewpoints. Several techniques, such as brainstorming and buzz sessions, are used to generate and exchange ideas as well as to solve problems. The following features are important to a quality group discussion:

❶ Your discussion begins with an introduction stating the purpose and objectives of the discussion.

❷ Everyone participates in the discussion; it is not dominated by one or two individuals.

❸ The discussion leads to an identified direction. You keep it on track and do not get off the subject.

❹ The discussion is focused on real-world problems.

❺ You set time limits for each phase of the discussion to ensure proportionate time is spent on each of the problems.

❻ You end the discussion with a summary of the main points and link it to previous learning and to future lessons.

DEMONSTRATION

A demonstration is an illustrated lecture or presentation that requires you to carry out a process step-by-step or series of actions so that trainees can observe and understand the procedure, principle, or phenomenon. This is often followed by having one of the trainees carry out the same activity under your guidance. It is a visual, practical presentation accompanied by discussion. Demonstrations have several advantages and disadvantages that you should consider.

Advantages of a Demonstration

1. You can appeal to trainees' verbal and visual modes of learning.

2. You can stimulate trainees' interest.

3. You can give trainees an expert model to follow.

4. You can control the pace and easily alter it to meet the needs of trainees. You can repeat the demonstration as many times as necessary.

5. You can relate principles taught in the classroom or through an instructor presentation, to real world situations.

6. You can give the trainees a chance to try the process under your supervision.

7. You can use the real object or a model of the real object.

Disadvantages of a Demonstration

1. A demonstration must be accurate, and therefore you must prepare and organise it very carefully. If things go wrong, you have lost the effect.

② It can be difficult for all trainees to see your demonstration well. You must limit a demonstration to small groups.

High quality, effective demonstrations have several common characteristics. Check to make sure your demonstrations have the following characteristics:

Characteristics of a Quality Demonstration

① Provide relevant information to trainees prior to the demonstration.

② Show and explain the procedure completely by going through the process step-by-step.

③ Perform the demonstration slowly enough so that trainees do not miss key points and you emphasise special techniques for doing a good job.

④ Look at and talk to your trainees not the equipment when you explain all new terms.

⑤ Be certain your demonstration is visible to all trainees.

⑥ Set up standards of quality and emphasise safe practices as you proceed.

⑦ Use common tools and equipment for the demonstration that the trainees will have access to.

⑧ Question trainees throughout the demonstration to ensure their understanding of each step and to get them to think through the job.

⑨ Watch for non-verbal clues, such as blank expressions, from the trainees that indicate how well they are following or responding to the demonstration.

10 Correct errors made by trainees trying the process.

11 Ask summarising questions to get feedback on how well trainees understood the demonstration.

READING

The reading method is an individualised approach to providing information to trainees. You give trainees printed materials or literature to read that contains the content to be learned or a series of procedures that must be mastered. There are several advantages and disadvantages of the reading method that you should consider.

Advantages of the Reading Method

1 It may save time. Trainees may be able to read faster than you can talk.

2 Trainees can save the material for later use.

3 Reading ensures that you present information consistently.

Disadvantages of the Reading Method

1 Reading can be boring to trainees if they must read too long without interruption.

2 Trainees read at different paces, so it is difficult to monitor group progress.

3 It is difficult to determine if trainees are learning and if reading assignments are actually completed.

Characteristics of a High Quality Reading Method

❶ The readings you select are directly related to the topic and contain important information. In some cases your readings should contain additional information not covered in class.

❷ The readings you select should be written at a level that the trainees can understand.

❸ Print should be large enough and dark enough so that trainees can read it easily.

EXERCISES

Exercises provide trainees with an opportunity to practice new skills that have been taught through another training method or to reinforce knowledge and skills that have been gained. Printed materials in the form of worksheets are commonly used. With recent advances in computer technology, personal computers are often used for various types of exercises. The following are some advantages and disadvantages for you to consider.

Advantages of Exercises

❶ Exercises help trainees remember what they have learned.

❷ Exercises allow trainees to practice new skills in a controlled environment.

❸ Trainees are actively involved in the learning process.

❹ Trainees may also learn other skills in the process of doing the exercises.

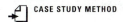

Disadvantages of Exercises

❶ You may have to spend extensive preparation time developing good exercises.

❷ It may be difficult for you to tailor exercises to meet all trainees' needs.

❸ Completing worksheets can take a lot of your training time.

❹ Trainees complete the exercises at different paces.

Characteristics Of High Quality Exercises

❶ Trainees clearly understand the purpose of the exercise and the directions for completing it.

❷ The exercises are difficult enough to challenge trainees but not so hard and time consuming that trainees lose interest and give up.

● At the end of the exercise you give trainees an opportunity to review what they have learned.

CASE STUDY

The case study gives a detailed account of an event or a series of related events. It may be presented to the trainees orally, in printed form, on overhead transparencies, video, flip chart, blackboard or a combination of these forms (multi-media presentation).

During a case study, you give trainees information about a situation and direct them to come to a decision or solve a problem concerning the situation. Case studies usually relate to real life situations and reduce the tendency of trainers to avoid real issues by talking about a theory rather than its application. Frequently, the major outcome of a case study is some type of product, such as a recommendation, a decision, or an action plan. Case studies can be brief or lengthy. You can have trainees work on case studies individually or in small groups. A discussion session usually follows the presentation of the case study. Case studies have a few advantages and disadvantages that you should consider.

Advantages of Case Studies

1. Case studies require active trainee involvement.

2. You can observe learning that is taking place.

3. Trainees often enjoy participating in case studies.

4. Case studies can help develop analytical and problem solving skills.

5. Case studies can be used by several small groups to generate a variety of solutions.

Disadvantages of Case Studies

1. Preparing quality case studies is difficult.

2. It is difficult to keep information precise and up-to-date.

3. Case studies can be very time consuming.

4. No definite solutions exist for the case study problems.

Characteristics of a High Quality Case Study

❶ Your case studies contain only essential facts, rather than extraneous facts and conditions that may confuse the trainees.

❷ In addition to necessary facts, your case studies describe important feelings and relationships of key individuals in the cases.

❸ Your case studies portray realistic situations and are of immediate concern to trainees.

❹ Events in the case take place according to an understandable time sequence.

❺ The problem is spelled out in specific terms for the trainees.

ROLE PLAY

In role playing, trainees act out a real life situation in front of an audience. During a role play, you give trainees information about a situation and ask them to perform as they would if it were a real life event. As there is no script or set dialogue, trainees make up their parts as they go along. This permits trainees to re-enact situations that they face on the job or in the future. The audience then attempts to apply the implications of the performance to the situation or problem being considered. Role plays have several advantages and disadvantages that you should consider.

Advantages of a Role Play

❶ Role plays can provide trainees with real life experiences.

❷ You can provide an opportunity to simulate performance required by trainees after the training.

❸ Role plays provides you an opportunity to portray hazardous or difficult settings without the risk.

❹ Trainees often find role plays to be motivating and fun.

❺ Role plays are effective ways of stimulating discussions that are aimed at problem solving.

Disadvantages of a Role Play

❶ If you do not organise and control the activity well, role plays can be viewed by trainees as a game and not a learning activity.

❷ If you do not plan properly, role plays may fail to make the intended points and no learning will occur.

❸ Developing quality role plays can require a great amount of your time.

❹ Role plays often involve only a few trainees rather than everyone.

Characteristics of a High Quality Role Play

❶ Trainees clearly understand the purpose of the role play.

❷ The plot or script of the role play is believable. It uses realistic characters, events, and procedures.

❸ All trainees are involved in the role play either as actors or audience. You give trainees who are not directly participating in the role play something to do (e.g., a checklist of things to watch for and give comments at the end of the role play).

❹ You summarise the role play by asking the trainees what they learned and provide feedback on their performances.

FIELD VISITS/STUDY TOURS

A field visit or study tour is a carefully arranged visit by a group to an object or place of interest for first hand observation and study. It can vary from a short visit to a single location to a trip or tour lasting several days and covering several states.

During a field visit or study tour, you give trainees an opportunity to see a situation for themselves. You can use a field visit or study tour by itself as a learning activity. However, it is usually more meaningful and effective for trainees if it is used to introduce a topic or to summarise a topic. If you use it as an introduction session, you are providing the background and real life setting needed for future lessons. You can also use the field visit or study tour to summarise what has been learned in the classroom and help trainees understand how it works in real life. A number of training methods and techniques and communication tools are used by the hosts during the field visits/study tour. Field visits have several advantages and disadvantages that you should consider.

Advantages of Field Visits/Study Tours

❶ Field visits provide trainees with an opportunity to see and experience things that can not be duplicated in the classroom. Trainees get to use all their senses (seeing, hearing, smelling, touching and tasting) as they learn.

❷ Field visits/study tours provide variety and a change of pace for trainees. They get both you and the trainees out of the routine of the class and the laboratory.

❸ Field visits/study tours provide the trainees with a common frame of reference. All trainees know exactly what is meant when the topic or location is discussed.

❹ Field visits/study tours can provide trainees with an opportunity to see how what they are learning can be used in real life.

Disadvantages of Field Visits/Study Tours

❶ Effective field visits/study tours require careful and time consuming planning.

❷ If you do not control the field visit/study tour, it can be viewed as a waste of time and not a learning activity.

❸ All trainees might not get the same learning experience.

❹ You can lose direct control over the learning experience if it is not properly organised.

Characteristics of Quality Field Visits/Study Tours

❶ Field visits/study tours should be highly structured and organised.

❷ Trainees should be required to turn in a written description of what they experienced. You can provide the questions to answer.

❸ Trainees do not just listen during the field visit/study tour. They are actively involved in the learning experience.

❹ Field visits/study tours should be directly related to learning objectives, and previous and future lessons.

Do not worry if you are unfamiliar with some of the training methods and techniques described above. If you are interested in learning more about these and other instructional strategies, there are a number of excellent publications which can provide you with the necessary information, and some are included at the end of this chapter. We suggest you read about these available and tested strategies and try them out in appropriate training situations. It has been proven that the more and varied the methods you use, the more learning will take place.

Selecting Training Methods

Major factors

Many things influence the selection or development of instructional procedures. However, there are five general factors you must take into consideration when you are selecting methods for your training. These factors are:

❶ The Training Objective
What are the proposed training outcomes? What are trainees expected to know or be able to do as a result of training? Does one method ensure reaching the objectives better than other methods?

❷ The Content
Depending on the subject matter to be covered, you opt for theoretically based or practically oriented methods.

❸ The Trainers
Are the trainers competent enough to use the various communication tools? Amount of experience, training in instructional methods, and formal education may be indicators of a trainer's competence.

❹ The Trainees
Does the method take into account group size, experience

SELECTING TRAINING METHODS

SECTION II / DEVELOPING CURRICULUM

levels, and other special characteristics of the trainees?

❺ The Practical Requirements
Is the method feasible given your physical environment, time (both preparation and actual training time), materials, and cost limitations?

THE TRAINING OBJECTIVE

Training objectives can stipulate that trainees understand something, do something they could not do before training, or change their attitudes or values. Each of these types of objectives requires different types of training methods.

Training for Understanding

If you want your trainees to "understand", furnish them with information using:

- Printed Materials
- Lectures/Instructor Presentations
- Diagrams
- Audiotapes and Videotapes
- Case Studies
- Demonstrations

To help trainees understand something, it is necessary for you to use training methods that allow you to review key points often, use relevant and realistic examples, and restate new ideas in different ways using familiar words and analogies.

Training for Skill Development

If you want your trainees to be able to do something new as a result of training, help them by using:

- Demonstrations
- Role Playing
- Videotapes
- Structured Exercises/Worksheets

To help trainees learn to do something new, it is necessary to use training methods that allow you to arrange for practice using the new skill, furnish positive and negative models and provide feedback as reinforcement.

Training for Changing Attitudes or Values

If you want your trainees to change their attitudes and values, assist them to inquire and observe the old versus the new, using:

- Demonstrations
- Field Visits/Study Tours
- Role Playing
- Case Studies
- Films and Videotapes
- Structured Games and Exercises
- Self-Analysis Instruments

To help trainees change their attitudes and values, it is necessary to use training methods that allow you to help them clarify old versus new attitudes and values, arrange opportunities to experiment with new values, and provide reinforcing links to solidify change over time.

 **SELECTING TRAINING METHODS**

SECTION II / DEVELOPING CURRICULUM

THE TRAINEES

When selecting a training method you should take into account the group size, experience levels, expectations, and other special characteristics of the group.

A reasonable rule of thumb for instructional group size is:

Instructor Presentations/Lectures	10 - 40 people
Demonstrations	3 - 10 people
Discussion Groups	3 - 10 people
Case Studies	3 - 20 people
Role Plays	5 - 15 people
Field Visits/Study Tours	5 - 25 people

The more experienced the trainees, the less you should use trainer centred training methods. The less experienced the trainees, the more appropriate are trainer centred methods. Examples of trainee centred training methods are group discussions, case studies, and role plays. As the trainer, you are less dominant when using these training methods. Trainees have more authority and responsibility for their learning than they do when you use a trainer centred method such as an instructor presentation. Your role becomes more of a facilitator where you set the boundaries for learning.

Trainees may have other special characteristics which you must consider when selecting training methods. For example you should consider the trainees' reading levels, their familiarity with each other, and their prior experience with different training methods. In general, it is a good idea for you to find out as much as possible about your trainees before training actually begins. Knowledge about special characteristics of the trainees will help you select appropriate training methods.

CHAPTER 6 / SELECT TRAINING METHODS AND TECHNIQUES

PRACTICAL REQUIREMENTS

Practical requirements relate to the feasibility of the training method given the physical environment, time constraints, available materials, and cost limitations. Practical requirements include such things as the seating arrangements available for training, the amount of noise and lighting in the training area, and the types of equipment, tools, and instructional materials that are available to you for training.

Procedure for Selecting Appropriate Training Methods

The following is a six step process designed to help you make good decisions regarding which training methods to select in different situations.

STEP 1.

State Training Objective

For each of the training objectives you have formulated, you should go through this procedure for selecting appropriate training methods.

STEP 2.

Determine performance indicated

Closely examine the objective as written. What performance are you looking for? Are you teaching for understanding? Are you teaching a skill? Are you attempting to change attitudes or values? You may find that for many objectives you are looking for multiple performances. For instance, to understand and be able to do.

STEP 3.

Consider trainee characteristics

You should find out as much as possible about the trainees prior to delivering instruction. How many trainees need training? How many trainees in each class? What educational levels are expected? How much work experience do trainees have related to the topic? What other important information about specific characteristics of the group do you have?

137

SECTION II / DEVELOPING CURRICULUM

STEP 4.

List appropriate training methods

The list of possible instructional procedures that can be used is almost endless. However, you do not have to know them all to make a good list. Chances are, if you are not familiar with a technique, you will not be able to use it effectively anyway. Just rely on your own and others' experience.

STEP 5.

Consider practical requirements

Consider the practical reality of your training situation. Where can training take place? What seating arrangements are possible? What is the environment of the training facility (lighting, noise, electricity, etc.)? What types of tools and equipment are available for training? What other important considerations and limitations exist? How much time do you have?

STEP 6.

Narrow the list and make final selection

At this point, you should compare the features and characteristics of the training methods you have selected. Choose the method that most closely approximates the conditions the trainees will encounter on the job and requires the trainees to practice what is called for by the objective. The most appropriate method is not always an available or practical option. If you determine that a number of methods would work equally well, select the one that is most available and with which you are most comfortable.

SELECTING TRAINING METHODS  CHAPTER 6 / SELECT TRAINING METHODS AND TECHNIQUES

BLANK SELECTING TRAINING METHODS WORKSHEET

TRAINING OBJECTIVE : ....

Performance Indicated:

Are you teaching for understanding?	YES	NO
Are you teaching a skill?	YES	NO
Are you attempting to change attitudes or values?	YES	NO

Trainee Characteristics:

How many trainees need training?
How many trainees in each class?
What educational levels are expected?
How much work experience is expected?
Other special characteristics?

Appropriate Training Methods:

Practical Requirements:

Where can training take place?
What seating arrangements are possible?
What is the environment of the training facility?

What types of tools and equipment are available?

Other important information?

Training Method(s) Selected:

 SELECTING TRAINING METHODS

SECTION II / DEVELOPING CURRICULUM

COMPLETED SELECTING TRAINING METHODS WORKSHEET

TRAINING OBJECTIVE :
Given coloured photographs of diseased plants, trainees will be able to correctly identify the disease and the severity of the symptoms.

Performance Indicated:

Are you teaching for understanding?	YES ✓	NO
Are you teaching a skill?	YES	NO ✓
Are you attempting to change attitudes or values?	YES	NO ✓

Trainee Characteristics:

How many trainees need training?	20
How many trainees in each class?	10
What educational levels are expected?	secondary school
How much work experience is expected?	less than 1 year
Other special characteristics?	reading difficulty

Appropriate Training Methods:

    instructor presentation with slide/tape;

    field visit

Practical Requirements:

Where can training take place?	classroom
What seating arrangements are possible?	any
What is the environment of the training facility?	must have a field site and two classrooms
What types of tools and equipment are available?	no audio visual equipment
Other important information?	electric power supply is erratic

---

Training Method(s) Selected:

    instructor presentation with photographs and flipcharts ;

    practical exercises in the field

Summary

This chapter has provided information to help you in the selection of, and planning for, the general training approach and the selection of specific training methods. Depending on your objectives, there are a number of training methods that are best suited for helping trainees achieve these objectives. It is important for you to be able to select the training methods that will best achieve your objectives.

Descriptions of several training methods, including advantages and disadvantages of each, were presented. The suggested procedure outlined in this chapter for selecting training methods involved making the decision based on five major factors: (1) the training objectives, (2) the content, (3) trainee characteristics, and (4) practical requirements. More specifically, a six step process was described to help you select appropriate training methods.

Additional References

Brown, James W., Lewis, Richard B., and Harcleroad, Fred F. (1983)
AV instruction: Technology, media, and methods.
New York : McGraw-Hill Book Co.

Craig, Robert L. (Ed.) (1987)
Training and development handbook: A guide to human resource development.
New York : McGraw-Hill Book Co.

Davies, Ivor K. (1981)
Instructional technique.
New York : McGraw-Hill Book Co.

Eitington, Julius E. (1984)
The winning trainer: Winning ways to involve people in learning.
Houston, London, Paris, Tokyo : Gulf Publishing Company Book Division.

Gagne, Robert M., Briggs, Leslie J., and Wagner, Walter W. (1988)
Principles of instructional design.
New York : Holt, Rinehart and Winston, Inc.

Laird, Dugan. (1985)
Approaches to training and development.
Reading, Massachusetts : Addison- Wesley Publishing Company, Inc.

The references below are very good if you are in a situation where access to, and production facilities for, training aids is limited.

Minor, Ed. (1962)
Simplified techniques for preparing visual instructional materials.
New York : McGraw-Hill Book Company, Inc.

Nelson, Leslie W. (1958)
Instructional aids and how to make them.
Dubuque, Iowa: William C. Brown Co.

Village technology handbook, Vols. 1 and 2.
Washington, D.C. : Department of State, Agency for International Development, Communications Resources Division.

CHAPTER 7

Develop training support materials

CHAPTER 7 / DEVELOP TRAINING SUPPORT MATERIALS

Overview

This chapter is focused on general guidelines for determining and finding needed materials for the implementation of a curriculum. Additionally, it provides suggestions and guidelines for developing some of the most important types of materials.

Training support materials for agriculture-related training are different from materials used in other sectors or in the schools of the world. In primary, secondary and higher education institutions, instructional materials are readily available. Since large numbers of students are being taught, governments, agencies, and commercial publishing companies are involved in developing and providing materials. However, with specific agricultural problems and needs, often limited to a region, country, or state, large numbers of people are not involved. The result is little attention is given to wide scale development of materials.

Agricultural development and training also require very current information to meet some needs and problems. Drought conditions in one region may require training and related support materials that have never been developed. Often, technical documents are available but they are not well suited to farmers. Consequently, trainers may find themselves in a situation where they must search for materials, adapt what they find, and/or develop some new materials to fit their training needs.

Training support materials may be of different types and forms. Essentially, training support materials are resources that, if used properly, will assist a trainer in accomplishing specific training objectives.

Types of Training Support Materials

Training support materials can vary greatly from simple, trainer constructed aids to complex, commercially produced materials. Trainers should be aware of both and should use what best meet their needs. The case, however, in many extension training situations is that com-

TYPES OF TRAINING SUPPORT MATERIALS

SECTION II / DEVELOPING CURRICULUM

mercially available materials that meet the specific training need are not available. Therefore, the trainer should be aware of the process for developing training support materials. The trainer should also be aware of the criteria that should be used to judge training support materials to ensure high quality.

Training support materials can be classified into two broad categories. These categories include:

❶ Printed materials, and

❷ Audio-visual materials.

PRINTED MATERIALS

Printed training support materials are materials that are printed on paper and usually carry a message that supports the training being conducted. These materials can be used to brief the training participant prior to training. Additionally, the materials can be used to reinforce one or more training methods used in the training course or session by providing the same message as in training but through a different medium, i.e., the printed word. Printed materials can also provide needed detail to what is covered in a training session. In this sense, the materials augment or add to the training. Also, printed materials can be used to reinforce learning and to summarise what has been covered.

Essentially, there are a number of prominent types of printed training materials. These include:

Handouts	Assignment Sheets
Learning Aids	Manuals
Workbooks	Study Guides
Technical References	Textbooks
Magazines/Journals	Pamphlets
Instructional Modules	Etc.

TYPES OF TRAINING SUPPORT MATERIALS

This list is not exhaustive but it contains the most common types of printed training support materials. There may be other names for pamphlet and references.

Advantages of Printed Training Support Materials

There are obvious advantages for the use of printed materials in the training setting. Some of these include:

❶ Print materials provide an alternative mode for transmitting information to the trainee. This can be in addition to a lecture, discussion or other training activity.

❷ Print materials can be easily reproduced within a short time period. They can also be distributed to larger number of trainees at a relatively cheaper cost.

❸ Print materials can be used in the future, beyond the training session. The materials can be used as a review or as reference materials.

❹ Print materials can communicate information that is in more depth than that provided during a training session. This can be useful for study before the training session or following the training session.

❺ Print materials can guide learning activities. Handouts and assignment sheets can focus the trainee on important content and learning experiences, thus improving the effectiveness and efficiency of the training experience.

❻ Some print materials can be used in self or independent learning. Self instruction modules or instructional pamphlets can be good learning tools.

TYPES OF TRAINING SUPPORT MATERIALS

SECTION II / DEVELOPING CURRICULUM

Limitations of Printed Training Support Materials

Printed materials also have limitations or disadvantages. These include:

❶ Print materials may not be tailored to the specific training situation and the objectives being pursued. Often, training materials may be available but they have been prepared for a generic situation of another, different training situation. The result may be an imperfect match with the training need.

❷ Print materials may not be well prepared. The preparation of training support materials requires a systematic and time consuming process. Often, as much time and expertise are necessary for preparing training materials as in the delivery of training. Sometimes materials are not of high quality.

❸ Reading level of printed training support materials is often inappropriate. Pamphlets, technical references and textbooks are often written at a high level, designed for scientists or subject matter experts. These materials may be inappropriate for farmers and others being trained. Moverover they may not be read at all if trainees have poor reading habits.

❹ Printed training materials may be very difficult to locate in many parts of the world. In developed nations it may be easier to locate materials than in developing countries. Even if they are available, they have to be adapted and translated into local language, and this takes time.

AUDIO - VISUAL MATERIALS

Audio-visual materials are training support materials that are used to augment various training methods. These materials usually rely on seeing or hearing, but may also rely on other senses for input. Audio-visual materials are used to clarify, emphasise and provide added information to lectures, demonstrations, group discussion and other methods. The materials in this category can be either trainer developed or commercially produced. However, most extension training involves trainer-produced materials. There are many types of audio-visual materials. The following list provides the most prominent ones:

Pictures	Flipcharts
Posters	Slides
Videotapes	Audiotapes
Overhead transparencies	Etc.

Advantages of Audio-Visual Training Support Materials

Several advantages and strengths of audio-visual materials are:

❶ Audio-visual materials provide for variety and motivation within the training session. They can help maintain the attention and interest of participants.

❷ Audio-visual materials provide an additional input for learning. Research on learning has shown that learning through more than one sense results in greater retention.

❸ Audio-visual materials can provide reality to the training by including pictures or renderings that can bring the field into the classroom.

❹ Audio-visual materials can contribute to faster understanding and message absorption.

❺ Audio-visual materials often give trainers added confidence in their delivery and this will also ensure consistency in delivery quality.

DEVELOPING TRAINING SUPPORT MATERIALS

SECTION II / DEVELOPING CURRICULUM

Limitations of Audio-Visual Training Support Materials

❶ Audio-visual materials are costly and require time, expertise, and production resources for their preparation.

❷ Many forms of audio-visual materials require equipment for their use. Overhead projectors, slide projectors, videotape players and other devices may be necessary. Unavailability of electrical power supply may limit the use of the equipment.

❸ Most audio-visual equipment require certain skills to handle them for effective presentation.

❹ Field settings may not be suited for production of audio-visual materials. Field processing, poster printing and other production may require central resources of large cities.

Developing Training Support Materials

The development of training support materials is a complex process. Each type of material has its own characteristics and procedure for development. Some general considerations are presented for print and audio-visual materials and a general procedure for their development is outlined. The process outlined may be applied to other materials.

STEP 1.

Establish the purpose for the materials

The purpose should be identified or determined as the first step in developing print and audio-visual materials. The purpose should relate directly to the objectives for which the materials will provide support. If the objectives are not evident for the materials, it is possible the materials are not needed.

Usually the purpose or aim of print and audio-visual materials is to provide background information, detailed explanation, or guide for practice or performance. Background information may be needed to provide the trainee with the proper context or setting prior to the training

DEVELOPING TRAINING SUPPORT MATERIALS

course. This allows the trainee to prepare themselves for the training, thus ensuring efficient use of training time.

Detailed information to support training is often a purpose of print materials. Training sessions are usually limited to the amount of time available. Consequently, a trainer can not cover every point of information that the trainee should learn. Print or audio-visual materials in the form of handouts or slide-tape sets can be used to provide additional information for the trainee to learn.

Training support materials can also have the purpose of providing guidance to the trainee in trying out or practising something that is being taught in the training course. An assignment sheet or a learning guide are examples. A guide might list the steps that are necessary to operate an implement or vehicle. The trainee can use this list to guide his or her practice.

STEP 2.
Identify the target audience

The users of print and audio-visual materials should be identified before the process of writing or development begins. Once the users or target audience are known, the materials can be targeted to the reading levels, knowledge levels and skill levels of the user.

Characteristics of the target audience that are identified in the needs assessment process can be useful in preparing training support materials. Also, by specifying the audience of the materials, other trainers may be able to make better decisions about the appropriateness of the materials for their training courses.

STEP 3.
Determine the type of material needed

The decision regarding the type of materials to produce should be directly related to the purpose of the materials and the training objectives being addressed. If materials are needed to orient or prepare the trainee for a training course, then the materials may take the form of a package of material that has been prepared to give the trainee an overview.

These materials may take the form of audio-cassette tape, brochure, booklet or small book. An alternative is a collection of articles or papers that are packaged together to form a booklet of readings or a slide-tape set.

Materials for use during instruction may take the form of handouts or learning guides. Handouts are usually short printed documents that relate to a specific topic being covered in the training. They are handed out so the trainee can either follow the text during instruction or they can use them outside the training setting for more indepth inquiry. They might also be useful in reviewing what has been learned.

Materials might also take the form of learning or job aids. These materials are designed to guide the trainee as he or she is trying a new task. They may list steps, ask questions to focus the trainee, or provide instructions on how to do something.

STEP 4.

Identify the Training Objectives that will be supported by the materials

The training objectives are the base of all training materials. The author of print or audio-visual materials must be very clear on what the instructional intent is. Once this is known, the author or writer should constantly check themselves to ensure that they are focusing on the objectives.

STEP 5.

Prepare an outline of the content

The content of the training support materials should be outlined. This outlining task should be based on a familiarity with the content that is gained through experience, experts or from reading other materials.

An outline specifies what will be included in the material. Additionally, it specifies the order in which topics are covered. Topics are usually dissected in the outline. That is, a topic is broken down into its subtopics.

The outline then forms a base from which sentences, paragraphs, and sections of the document can be written.

STEP 6.

Organise the Material to facilitate use and learning

The outline actually specifies the order of the major segments of content. However, within topics and subtopics there are several principles that can be followed in writing materials. These include:

Simple to complex. Information should be presented in simple terms first with little complexity. Pieces of a process are first described before showing the interrelationships that exist. The parts of an implement are first described before describing the operation of the implement.

Known to unknown. In writing about a new process, it is advantageous to describe or relate to a similar process that the trainees already know about. This establishes a set or orientation and gives the trainee something to build upon with the new information.

Concrete to abstract. Material should begin with concepts and processes that are fairly concrete and straight forward. Then, these materials can go into principles and concepts that may be more theoretical and abstract.

STEP 7.

Make the Material attractive

Attention should be paid to making the materials attractive to the person who will use them. Many times, it takes little effort and expense to improve the looks of instructional materials. Using a good typewriter, a microcomputer and good quality printer along with good quality duplicating equipment can greatly enhance the appearance of materials.

The attractive document gives the user a greater feeling of importance toward the training and may be more likely to read, respect, and use the material.

STEP 8.

Pretest prototype training materials

In order to ensure that trainees correctly interpret, perceive and understand the meaning of the messages or contents contained in training materials, a pretesting exercise would be very useful and should be undertaken. Important training materials, including teaching aids and learning materials, shuold be developed and packaged as prototypes to be pretested before final production with a small sample of the actual target audience. A message pretesting exercise can be done in a very short time with limited cost and simple methodology, and may rresults in a significant improvement in the effectiveness of the training materials as well as a considerable saving of resources (time, effort and funds). Such a formative evaluation of training materials (i.e. messages or contents) prior to the actual implementaion of training activity should thus be considered as a built-in or integral part in a training materials design, development and production process.

Summary

Training support materials should be utilised where additional emphasis or reinforcement is needed for the subject matter being presented. The various types of support materials, particularly the audio-visual, may allow the trainer to present information in a more dynamic, and interesting manner.

The trainees may be provided with written matter that can provide more detailed information that time would not allow to be presented during the formal class sessions. Written matter may also be utilised to reinforce topics covered in class, and these materials will be in the hands of the trainees so that in the future they may refer to them as they wish.

Additional References

FAO (1990)
Make Learning Easier: A Guide to improving educational/ training materials.
Rome, Italy: Food and Agriculture Organization (FAO) of the United Nations.

IRRI (n.d.)
Designing and Producing Instructional Media and Materials.
Los Baños, the Philippines: Training & Technology Transfer Dept., International Rice Research Institute (IRRI).

Crone, Catherine D. and Hunter, Carman St. John (1980)
From the Field: Tested Participatory Activities for Trainers.
New York: World Education.

Develop tests for measuring trainee learning

CHAPTER 8

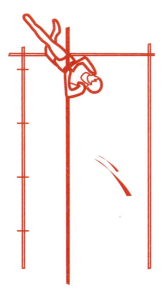

OVERVIEW

CHAPTER 8 / MEASURING TRAINEE LEARNING

Overview

Measuring the extent of learning is an important but often overlooked aspect of training by the person who develops the curriculum. Measurement in the training context refers to the process of quantifying (or assigning a number) what someone knows or can do. For example, in *Chapter 3*, you were instructed on assessing the current skill levels of trainees by giving specific tasks a rating. That was a form of measurement. The process of testing is another, possibly the most common, form of measurement in training.

The measurement of trainee learning has several purposes and uses. These uses can be emphasised within training situations and it is possible to pursue more than one use at a time.

❶ **To emphasise important content.** By including a particular knowledge or skill element in a test or other measuring tool, the trainer can bring emphasis to that element. This may provide for review and summary as well as measuring acquisition of the knowledge or skill.

❷ **To facilitate learning of training content.** The use of tests and measures sends an important message to trainees: that they will be evaluated. This fact, for many trainees, makes them pay greater attention to the course content and may motivate them to review and study the content outside of the instructional setting.

❸ **To reveal areas of trainee weakness or limited learning.** Tests and other measures can indicate how well trainees have mastered the course objectives. If the trainer discovers that not all have mastered an objective, or that many may be having trouble with one or more elements of content, the trainer can use this information to design remedial activities. For example, if a test reveals that trainees are having difficulty in identifying pest damage to a crop sample, the trainer could spend additional time on that topic.

161

❹ To assist in the evaluation of the training course. Trainee learning results can provide the trainer and the sponsors of the training an indication of training success. This information may be useful in making decisions about delivering the course in other settings, about replacing the training with something else, or about making an investment in revising the training.

❺ To aid in curriculum revision. Test or measurement results can identify parts of the curriculum that are weak. If trainees are having difficulty in learning, this may indicate the need to revise the curriculum and training plan to incorporate new and different content.

These are potential purposes for measuring the achievement of intended learning outcomes. These should be considered as one is designing a training curriculum and measuring the learning of trainees. Before a test or measuring instrument is developed, you should first answer the following two questions: "Why am I measuring trainee learning?" and "What will I do with the results of the measurement?" The answers to these questions will clarify your purpose(s) for measurement.

Types of Tests and Measurement Tools for Training

Testing and measurement are complex activities and have many different forms and procedures. Some countries do nation-wide testing. This type of testing requires a very elaborate development and validation procedure. Trainers, however, seldom have the time and resources to undergo such elaborate test development. Consequently, trainers engage in simplified measurement procedures that meet their specific needs. The following paragraphs identify the most appropriate and useful types of measuring tools for trainers.

Paper and Pencil Tests

Paper and pencil tests are designed primarily to measure knowledge related achievement or learning. They are efficiently developed by trainers and curriculum developers and can meet many of the purposes cited above. Their development is based on course objectives, elements of objectives, or content outlines. They may include a variety of test item types that include: 1) True-False, 2) Multiple Choice, 3) Matching, 4) Short Answer, and 5) Essay. Each of these item types has distinct advantages and disadvantages for the measurement of a particular type of learning. For example, a true-false item can measure recall or recognition of learned facts but it cannot measure understanding of a complex process. The essay item is much better at measuring more complex learning.

Performance Tests

Performance tests are focused on measuring the skills of trainees. While most skills have knowledge elements, just having the knowledge doesn't mean someone can perform the skill adequately. For example, someone might know all the parts of a tank sprayer, might be able to list all necessary steps in filling and using it to spray herbicides, and may be able to recite the important safety considerations related to the sprayer. However, the person may not be able to actually fill and appropriately use the sprayer. Therefore, in measuring skill we must focus on performance as well as knowledge.

Performance tests fall in two broad categories:

❶ identification tests, and

❷ work samples or simulations.

Each measure has its own special purposes and applications.

Planning a Test or Measuring Tool

The planning of a test or measuring tool is very similar to the planning of anything: it requires advance thought and organisation. Planning a test should begin with the intent and content of the training course. This can include the course objectives and the content outline that have been portrayed in the training plan.

In reviewing the training plan for the listing of objectives and course content, you will quickly realise that there may be far too much content to cover in a test or measuring tool. Since this is the case, we must sample or select only a segment of the content to include in the measurement exercise. This sampling or selection of the content to include in the test is a critical step. The following procedure is designed to help you in the planning of a test.

STEP 1.

Determine the segment of training you wish to include in the test

This decision is somewhat arbitrary and dependent on the purpose(s) you have chosen for the test. If you are delivering a week long course you might test midway through the course and at the end of the course. If you are delivering a six week course, you might administer a test at the end of each week. Or, if you are teaching a highly skill oriented course, you might administer a measuring tool for each of the major skills that are included in the course, regardless of when they occur.

PLANNING A TEST OR MEASURING TOOL

CHAPTER 8 / MEASURING TRAINEE LEARNING

Fig. 8.1   SAMPLE TABLE OF SPECIFICATIONS FORMS

Objectives	Relative Emphasis	TYPES OF LEARNING			Item Totals
		Knowledge	Attitude	Skill	
❶ In an appropriate field setting, the students will be able to perform and interpret nitrate, phosphate, and potash plant tissue tests consistent with tissue testing practices	20%	4	0	1	5
❷ to ❽ (other objectives related to the same topic area	80%	12	3	4	19

Source: Agriculture Bulletin #723

STEP 2.

Review the content of the course segment you have selected and write in on the Table of Specifications Form

A table of specifications is a form that can guide your development of a test or measuring tool. It provides a mechanism for identifying needed test items and it assures a proper balance in the test. Essentially, in this step you should list the course objective being addressed then present the knowledge, skill and attitude elements that are related to the objective. This means listing the major topics of training from the outline in the appropriate column of the table of specifications. See Fig. 8.1. for a sample form of such a table.

STEP 3.

Determine the relative emphasis of each content element

This step should involve a determination or recording of how much of the course is devoted to each segment of the course. Stated another way, indicate how important or critical each segment is. This can be accomplished by reviewing task analysis information or by simply making a judgement based on how much time is spent on the segment of training. The sample form provided, asks you to indicate the proportion or percentage of the course that you have devoted to each segment.

It should be obvious that the test used in a course should reflect the content of the course and in the correct proportion. It would be inappropriate to devote 40% of a test to a segment of the course that was only 10% of the total. The table of specifications assists you in this regard.

STEP 4.

Identify the needed type of instrument and the needed types of test items for each segment of content

Using the information presented in the next sections of this chapter, select the approach and item types that can best meet the testing need and purpose. Placing a tick in the appropriate column provides an indication of what is needed.

After the table of specifications is complete, you have a detailed plan to guide your test development. By following this plan you should be able to determine what type of test item is needed for each content element and how much emphasis should be provided in the overall test.

Paper and Pencil Tests of Knowledge

Testing the learning of knowledge is the most common of all testing. Knowledge testing is the easiest and most efficient and that accounts for its common use. However, trainers should take caution to give appropriate emphasis to knowledge, skill and attitude. Of course, the test plan or table of specifications will assist in this process.

A knowledge test is made up of a series of test items. Test items are questions or statements that ask the trainee to respond in some way. There are two basic categories of knowledge test items: recognition items and constructed response items.

RECOGNITION ITEMS

Recognition items require the trainee to be presented with a stimulus, usually in the form of a question or a declarative statement, and make a response by choosing a correct response. Since the trainee sees the alternate choices, he or she must recognise the correct or appropriate one. The recognition item has many advantages. The primary advantages are related to the capability to measure a broad range of learning and the extreme efficiency in scoring the test. These advantages make recognition items the most popular in measuring knowledge learning.

The three major types of the recognition item are the multiple choice item, the true-false item and the matching item. Each of these has its own use in testing knowledge. The following paragraphs provide a description of each of these recognition items along with suggestions for their development.

Multiple Choice Items

Multiple choice items are the most common of all test items. A multiple choice item consists of a stimulus statement, usually called an item stem, followed by a list of four or five possible responses or alternatives. The item stem may be in the form of an incomplete sentence or a direct question. In all cases, however, only one of the alternatives should be correct. The remaining alternatives should be incorrect and are often referred to as distractors.

The following suggestions provide a base for developing multiple choice items.

SUGGESTION 1.

Formulate an item stem using simple and concise language

The item stem must be direct and contain a single concept or question. It should not be wordy. The trainee should be able to read the stem and gain a clear picture of what is being asked without struggling with the language. It is also suggested that the stem be worded positively. That is, ask "What is the best material for building crop storage?" rather than, "What material is not the best for building crop storage?"

SUGGESTION 2.

Construct plausible and unambiguous alternatives

Alternatives to a particular item stem should appear equally attractive to the unknowledgeable trainee. The alternatives should be grammatically consistent with the stem. Also, you should be cautious not to make the correct response stand out from the others because you attempt to ensure it is the best choice. For example, don't make the correct alternative longer (contain more words) than the incorrect alternatives.

Additional suggestions for writing alternatives deal with placement of the correct alternative and use of generalisations. Be cautious not to put the correct response in the same place for all items. For example, don't make the "a" response the correct one on all items, vary the placement. Also, don't use generalising alternatives such as "all of the above" or "none of the above".

SUGGESTION 3.

Review and revise items prior to their use

The process of developing multiple choice items is difficult and time consuming. It is important to develop items in a systematic way and to review each one after they are all developed. This should help in identifying ways to improve the items. Another suggestion is to have a colleague or fellow trainer review the items that you have written and ask him or her to suggest ways of improving the items.

Example Multiple Choice Item

At what point in time should whole grain be introduced in rations for pigs?
(Please circle the appropriate answer.)

a. At age 3 months
b. Usually at 14 days
c. As soon as they will eat it
d. As soon as they can move about

True-False Items

True false items are the easiest item type to develop. They are straight forward statements of fact that the trainee must mark as either true or false. The true false item is exceptionally well suited to identifying the correctness or accuracy of definitions, terms, statements of principles and statements of facts.

The true false item has several advantages. The item is easy and efficient to score. That is, a trainer or assistant can very quickly determine the correctness of a series of true false items. The true false item can provide for the sampling of a broad segment of course content. Since most training has a basic knowledge component, true false items can be developed for some aspect of the entire course. A third advantage is the ease of constructing true false items. Compared to other item types the true false item is easily and quickly developed.

There are two major shortcomings or disadvantages of the true false item. First, the true false item can only measure factual knowledge and not more complex knowledge such as understanding and problem solving. Second, the true false item, because it has only two choices, has a high probability for guessing correctly. Trainees may guess and thus not give a true representation of what they know.

The following suggestions are provided to guide you in the development of true-false items.

SUGGESTION 1. **Avoid general statements**	General statements often have qualifying words that give away the correct response to the item. Example words include: generally, often, sometimes, usually, always, never, all, none, and only. The trainee may see these words and be able to choose the correct response without knowing the true content of the item.
SUGGESTION 2. **Avoid over-simplification**	When attempting to make statements definitely true or clearly false, one may select content that is not directly related to the course objective and knowledge elements. Also, one should avoid using direct quotes from books or training materials. This may encourage the memorising of text rather than learning.
SUGGESTION 3. **Present a single idea in the true false item**	It is important to avoid including two or more ideas or statements within the same item. If there are two or more parts in an item, the trainee may know the correctness of one and not the other, thus incorrectly responding to the item. The result is a misinterpretation of the trainees knowledge.

SUGGESTION 4.

Avoid the use of negative terminology and especially double negatives

Many times the terms such as no or not are overlooked by the trainee and result in an incorrect response to the item. In special cases negative terminology may be necessary. In these cases you should bring attention to the negative word(s) by underlining or making it bold.

SUGGESTION 5.

Avoid the use of unfamiliar language and terminology

With most true false items, the intention is to assess trainee's knowledge of the content area and not vocabulary that is outside the content area. Therefore, it is very important to include only familiar terms that are related to the training.

SUGGESTION 6.

Attempt to make the length of all true false items equal

There is often a tendency to make the true items longer than false items. This can be sensed by some trainees and it may give them an unfair advantage on the test.

SUGGESTION 7.

Include approximately the same number of true and false items in the test

This should be attempted to ensure that trainees do not expect more true than false or visa versa.

These suggestions are presented to guide you in the development of good true false items. The key point to remember in writing true false items is to base them on your table of specifications or test plan. Because true false items are easy to develop, they often get over used at the expense of testing other important content and skills.

Example True and False Items

1. Pesticides are the solution to the problem of flying insects in rice farming.
   .... True   .... False

2. Natural control of insects is possible in most situations.
   .... True   .... False

Matching Items

A third type of recognition item is the matching item. Actually, the matching item is a special form of a multiple choice item. While the multiple choice item comprised an item stem and a series of alternatives, the matching item has a series of stems and a series of alternatives. Matching items are usually presented in two columns: one for stems and one for alternatives.

The matching item can be used to measure the trainees knowledge of associations. The objectives that emphasise the identification of relationships can often be assessed through the matching item. Examples of relationships that can be measured with the matching item include:

1. Inventor - Inventions

2. Tools - Applications

3. Machines - Uses

4. Plant diseases - Treatments

5. Symbols - Concepts

❻ Terms - Definitions

❼ Plants - Classifications

❽ Problems - Solutions

A primary advantage of the matching item lies in its efficiency. It can measure a broad array of content with very little time required of the trainee. The item takes a small amount of space on the test and it is easily scored or graded. The major disadvantages lie in the difficulty of obtaining a sufficient amount of content from one general area for including in the item and the limitation of the item to mostly factual information.

The following suggestions are offered to assist you in developing matching items for written tests.

SUGGESTION 1. **Use only homogeneous material**	Content material used in formulating both stem and alternatives must come from the same general area or domain and must match up with your test plan. The content must be similar in order that all alternatives are plausible for each item stem.
SUGGESTION 2. **Formulate clear and concise directions**	The directions for the matching item should be presented immediately preceding the item. The directions should inform the trainee exactly what is expected of them. If the trainee is allowed to use one alternative more than once, this should be indicated in the directions. The directions should also indicate to the student how they should record their responses, e.g. write the letter of the alternative next to the stem, etc.
SUGGESTION 3. **Keep the number of items and alternatives small**	Ten elements in a matching item is usually the maximum. Longer items are both difficult for the trainee to deal with and difficult for the trainer to develop.

SUGGESTION 4.

Include more alternatives than items

To decrease the trainees' chance of guessing correctly on the basis of elimination, columns should be of unequal length. If the columns are equal, the last choice is made with no decision - it is the only one left.

SUGGESTION 5.

The entire item should be included on a single page

It is much easier for the trainee to make their choices if they do not have to turn a page to view the total list of alternatives.

SUGGESTION 6.

Place the lists of items and alternatives in a logical order

Alphabetical, numerical sequence, chronological, and so on are options for ordering the items and alternatives.

These suggestions provide general guidance in preparing a matching item. Most tests use a small number of matching items (one or two) and augment them with other types of recognition and constructed response items.

Example Matching Items

Match the applications in column two with the tools in column 1. Write the letter of the application next to the tool in column 1.

TOOLS

... 1. Pliers
... 2. Screwdriver
... 3. Side Cutter
... 4. Aviation shear
... 5. Lug wrench

APPLICATIONS

a. Tighten screws
b. Splice wire
c. Cut sheet metal
d. Cut wire
e. Raise vehicle
f. Loosen wheel bolts
g. Drill a hole

CONSTRUCTED RESPONSE ITEMS

The constructed response item is the second major classification of items used to measure knowledge learning. Basically, as its name implies, the constructed response item includes a stimulus of some kind to which the trainee must construct or write a response. There are two types of constructed response items: short answer and essay. The following paragraphs present an overview of each of these item types and suggestions for their development.

Short Answer Items

Short answer items take three forms: completion, definition, and identification. The completion item is simply an incomplete sentence that the trainee must complete with a word or phrase to make it correct. The definition item requires the trainee to write the definition of a term. The third type of short answer item is focused on assessing a trainees knowledge of certain objects. They usually involve showing a diagram, drawing or picture and the trainee must identify what it is and write down its name.

The short answer item has several advantages. It can be used to measure knowledge of facts, principles and processes. This is more than what most recognition items can do. Second, with the short answer item it is difficult for the trainee to guess correctly. The major disadvantage of the short answer item lies in its scoring or grading. Unlike the recognition item, the short answer item may have many different responses that may be correct. With more than one word meaning the same thing, the grader of such an item must be able to make judgments regarding the acceptability of answers. This is usually time consuming and difficult.

The following paragraphs provide suggestions for developing short answer items.

SUGGESTION 1.

Require short and concise answers

The question should be worded precisely and focused appropriately to ensure a short response. The amount of space included for a response can also be a sign to the trainee that only a short answer is desired.

SUGGESTION 2.

Completion items should have singular completing words or phrases

Avoid leaving more than one blank to be filled in. The stem must include sufficient detail to inform the student of what is expected in the response.

SUGGESTION 3.

Avoid using direct statements from books or training materials

It is usually better to identify a concept or idea and paraphrase it for a short answer item than to use verbatim statements.

SUGGESTION 4.

Allow for synonyms or similar answers in the scoring or grading key

In developing a scoring key, all possible correct responses should be included. Also, as you score the tests, you should remain flexible in identifying new responses that are appropriate.

Example Short Answer Items

1. Define the term "Field Monitoring".

2. The best type of grain storage in North India is the . . . .

These suggestions will assist you in developing effective short answer items. Even though more difficult to score than recognition items, the short answer items minimise guessing and they allow you to measure more advanced knowledge learning.

Essay Items

The essay item requires the trainee to write a response using his or her own words. This item type is usually focused on assessing objectives that require the student to recall, organise, and present ideas. The essay item should be used to measure more than factual knowledge. It is capable of measuring higher order knowledge skills.

Essay items can vary in terms of their breadth and length. They can require a paragraph response or a three page response. The purpose and underlying objective should be the key in determining length.

The major advantage of the essay item is the type of learning that can be measured as mentioned above. Additionally, the essay item is easy to develop. The biggest disadvantage of the essay item is in its scoring or grading. The essay item requires a great deal of time to read each answer. Also, the essay item requires judgement in determining the degree of correctness in a trainees response.

The following suggestions are provided to guide you as you develop essay items.

SUGGESTION 1.

Use essay items to measure knowledge that you can not measure with any other item type

Because of the difficulty in grading essay items, they should be used for those content elements that you cannot measure with recognition or short answer items.

SUGGESTION 2.

Include specific directions to the trainee

The trainee should know enough about the trainers expectations to be able to approach the problem and answer the question adequately. There should be no attempt to trick the student.

SUGGESTION 3.

Indicate the approximate time limit for each essay item

This estimate should be based on the amount of time the trainer thinks should be spent on the item. This gives the trainee an idea of how much time to spend on this item compared to other items in the test.

SUGGESTION 4.

Limit the use of optional items

Some trainers provide three essay items and allow the trainees to select and respond to two of the three. This practice makes it difficult to grade tests and to compare students since not all will have completed the same items.

SUGGESTION 5.

An ideal answer should be written before an item is included

The formulation of an ideal response can provide an indication of the reasonableness of the item. Also and estimate of time can be derived for the item. A grading key can also be developed through this process.

Example Essay Item

Identify and discuss four factors that have an impact on the agriculture economy of your country.

This section has provided suggestions for developing essay items. These items are exceptionally useful in measuring higher order knowledge and should be used when the test plan calls for them.

The measurement of knowledge is an important process. This chapter segment has provided an overview of the general types of knowledge measurement and the types of items that can be used. By following the test plan or table of specifications, an extremely useful test can be developed.

Developing a Performance Test

Performance measurement or testing in training is concerned with the assessment of skills, usually motor skills or physical actions. Because of the time and effort necessary to develop and implement good performance tests, they have not been used extensively. However, a majority of training done in agriculture and agriculture extension has the objective of improved skills and practices. Therefore, performance testing should be considered as part of an effective training programme.

In measuring performance, it is possible to focus on both the process and the product of a given task. For example, in measuring a farmer's skill at filling and adjusting a tank sprayer, you could focus on how well he or she follows the expected procedures (process) and you could observe the tank sprayer and determine if it has been filled and adjusted properly (product). Both of these points are important.

The process of a task can be measured through observation and the use of a checklist. Product measurement can be accomplished by judging the result of the task by observing the product and judging its quality.

Performance tests have both advantages and disadvantages. The primary advantage of the performance test lies in its ability to assess complex behaviours in a realistic situation. It also, generally, has high validity and credibility. The greatest disadvantage of performance tests is in the time and effort required to develop and administer the test. This time is critical to both trainer and trainees.

TYPES OF RATING SYSTEMS AND INSTRUMENTS

Rating of performance is a common act in the testing of performance. Ratings can comprise of either the processes that trainees demonstrate or the products they produce. In either case the object of the rating need not be large or complex. The skills of welders are assessed by rating the welds they make. The performance of typists is judged by rating the documents they produce. The performance of farmers in enacting a new skill is made through observation and rating.

Essentially, there are three types of rating systems. These include: instructor or supervisor ratings, peer ratings, and self ratings. *Instructor or supervisor ratings* are completed by a trainer or a work supervisor who assumes the responsibility for observing someone perform a task. They use some form of checklist or rating scale to guide their rating and to record their results.

Peer rating involves trainees evaluating each other and each others products. These ratings are also guided and assisted by a rating instrument.

Self rating is also a key means for judging performance. An individual can use a rating scale to judge the quality of their product and result. Self ratings are often the best means of rating since they facilitate and encourage self improvement without someone else needing to require change or improvement.

There are several different instruments that can be used to assist performance measurement. These include checklists and rating scales.

Checklist is the simplest of rating instruments. Checklist includes a list of behaviours or activities that are important to the proper completion of a task. They can also be focused on the critical features of a product. The user of a checklist (trainer, supervisor, peer or trainee) observes either

DEVELOPING A PERFORMANCE TEST

process or product and places a tick next to the items on the checklist that are observed. Items that do not receive a tick are determined to be deficiencies or weaknesses. By adding the check marks or ticks, a score for the performance can be computed.

Example Checklist

Tank Sprayer is to:

.... Release pressure from tank
.... Rotate handle counter clockwise
.... Pull out pump assembly
.... Rinse chemical from tank with water
.... Flush pump and line with water

A more sophisticated use of the checklist for process, involves recording both the observation of an action as well as its correct sequence. For example, a checklist focused on determining the proper cleaning of a tank sprayer would include all the necessary steps. As the rater makes the observation of a trainee in the act of cleaning a sprayer, he or she would record the first step taken, the second step taken, the third step and so on. The results can be very useful in judging one's skill as well as in providing corrective instruction.

Rating scales measure characteristics by assigning numbers to specific rating categories. For example, a trainer might use a rating scale to measure a trainees ability to use a soil sampling kit. The rating scale might range from 1 to 5 with 5 being the best. The rating scale relies on the observation and judgemental skill of the rater. An adaptation of the rating scale is to add descriptive words to the numbers. For example, 1 equals poor, 3 equals adequate, and 5 equals excellent. Words make the ratings more reliable or consistent. By adding and averaging the ratings on a specific task or activity, the trainer can gain a general indication of performance.

Example Rating Scale Segment

Rate the trainees performance on the following:

	poor				excellent
Coordination	1	2	3	4	5
Attention	1	2	3	4	5
Attitude	1	2	3	4	5

MAJOR TYPES OF PERFORMANCE TESTS

There are three major types of performance tests. These include: identification tests, work sample and simulation tests, and supervisor ratings.

Identification Tests

Identification tests are designed to assess a trainee's ability to identify objects or parts of objects, to distinguish between correct and incorrect procedures, to identify basic elements of a process, and to identify the adequacy of products. Identifying a specific tool by name when shown, asking the trainee to identify the correct procedure when observed, or selecting the best product from a set of products, are all examples of identification tests. These tests can involve paper and pencil for recording responses or they can be administered orally.

The following procedures are suggested for developing an identification test.

DEVELOPING A PERFORMANCE TEST

CHAPTER 8 / MEASURING TRAINEE LEARNING

STEP 1. Identify the desired behaviour	Before any test is developed, it is necessary to define very specifically what is to be measured. The table of specifications referred to in an earlier section of this chapter helps ensure relevance. If a table of specifications has not been prepared, a review of your training plan and/or the task analysis information you collected can be useful in determining what to test.
STEP 2. Select items or products to be included in the identification test	Based on the result of step 1, objects should be located and obtained for the test. If the important skill is to identify the parts of a tank sprayer, you would obtain and disassemble a tank sprayer. If you use a paper and pencil version of an identification test, then you would draw or produce photographs of the sprayer parts.
STEP 3. Develop an operating plan for the test	An operating plan provides the general organisation for the test. It states how things should be set up or displayed, how trainees should be instructed, and how performance will be judged.
STEP 4. Develop and reproduce a recording form and other related documents	Developing a recording form or answer sheet is a simple task. It should be designed to make it easy to score and assign a rating or grade for the performance.
STEP 5. Develop instructions for the test	A necessary component for any test is directions to the trainee on how to respond and record one's choices. The physical arrangements for the test and the size of the group being tested will determine the need for detail in the instructions.

STEP 6.

Try out and revise the test

The tryout of the test can occur in two stages. The first phase involves a small scale simulation of the actual test with a small number of trainees. This tryout can help test the operating procedures, directions, recording form and products themselves. The second phase involves the first administration of the test to a regular group of trainees. This will reveal any real problems that can be corrected before the next time the test is used.

Work Sample and Simulation Tests

A work sample test of performance is a controlled test that is administered using the actual conditions of the job. It is a segment or sample of an actual job (although the test may not be given on the job). The trainee is required to use exact procedures that would be used in the work situation.

Simulation tests are tests designed to duplicate or simulate the real life work situation by using special equipment for testing or making modifications in existing equipment.

Having trainees plan and implement a pest control system for their farm with close observation by a trainer, is an example of a work sample. Having trainees manipulate the pieces of a farm model in executing a cultivation test is an example of a simulation.

The complexity of the task being assessed and access to testing facilities and equipment will have a great deal to do with the procedures that will be used in the work sample or simulation test. However, there are general steps that will aid you in developing a test.

STEP 1.

Select a sample of the job or occupation

The job and task analysis results can be very useful in identifying the sample. The job sample should focus on behaviours that are important, frequently used, or difficult to measure with paper and pencil tests.

STEP 2.

Develop a rating or recording form

Once a job segment and corresponding tasks or qualities to be included in the performance test have been selected, the next step is to determine the important features of the process or product of performance. From these, a rating scale should be developed.

STEP 3.

Survey practical limitations of testing environment

Knowing the practical limitation of testing is important so you can either overcome or avoid the limitations. Limitations include: time for testing, people needed to supervise, and availability of facilities and equipment.

STEP 4.

Develop an operating plan

The operating plan should include an outline or set of directions for the set up and conduct of the performance test. This should include: directions for the trainer, directions for the trainee, directions for checking the conditions of equipment and directions for overall conduct of the test.

STEP 5.

Try out and revise the test

The work sample or simulation test should be placed into action for a trial run to help identify problems in procedures, rating forms, and the testing environment. Based on the test, changes and improvements should be made.

The use of performance tests in training is very important. They provide a valid and credible way to determine if the trainees can do what you intend for them to do. The performance test comes closer to the real world than any other type of test. However, they have their costs in terms of facility, equipment and time.

SUMMARY

SECTION II / DEVELOPING CURRICULUM

Summary

The measurement of trainee learning is a critical step in the training function. Many trainers believe that their task is complete when the actual training is over. However, measurement of learning can contribute to better training and better performance.

Testing can be conducted by using either paper and pencil measures of intellectual skills or observation oriented performance tests. Each has its place and should be selected based on the situation and need. The results of measurement can be used to help trainers, trainees, and sponsors of training.

Additional References

Erickson, Richard C., and Wentling, Tim L. (1988)
Measuring Student Growth, Techniques and Procedures for Occupational Education.
Urbana, Illinois : Griffon Press.

Gronlund, N. E. (1981)
Measurement and Evaluation in Teaching.
New York : MacMillan.

Raab, Robert T., Swanson, Burton E., Wentling, Tim L., and Clark, Charles D. (1991)
Improving Training Quality: A Trainer's Guide to Evaluation.
Food and Agriculture Organization of the United Nations : Rome, Italy.

Wiersma, W., and Jurs, S. G. (1985)
Educational Measurement and Testing.
London : Allyn and Bacon, Inc.

Tryout and revise the curriculum

CHAPTER 9

9

Trypus and Ivyffe
the curriculum

OVERWIEV

CHAPTER 9 / TRYOUT AND REVISE THE CURRICULUM

Overview

The tryout, or pretest as it is commonly called, of the curriculum and its associated parts is important for several reasons. Like most important products that are newly developed, it is important to test the curriculum to ensure that it works as it was intended to work. A tryout or pretest of the curriculum can provide evidence to show that it contains appropriate content and is organised in the optimal way.

The pretest of the curriculum can also help in identifying parts of the curriculum that may need to be changed or improved prior to full-scale implementation. The pretest might point out that an incorrect method was selected for teaching part of the course, that not enough time was allotted for a field visit, or that the printed materials were inappropriately designed. By learning about problems such as these early in the implementation process, changes and corrections can be made to ensure smooth and effective delivery of the course.

The tryout of the curriculum can also be used to build confidence in the curriculum. The instructor, by being involved in a pretest, can become knowledgeable and comfortable with the course. Then, when full implementation begins, the instructor can smoothly execute the curriculum plan. Confidence in the curriculum can also be gained by potential participants and by sponsors of the course if they know the curriculum has been pretested and revised.

The tryout of the curriculum can take various forms. It can include a professional judgement by subject matter experts, curriculum specialists or trainers. Any of these individuals can be asked to review and critique course materials and lesson plans. Tryout can also involve implementation of the curriculum on a small scale, perhaps with only several students. These students could be debriefed or interviewed during and after instruction to gain their insights into the strengths and weaknesses of the course. Of course, instructors may provide a great

191

deal of feedback about the curriculum, either as reviewers or as participants in implementation.

Tryout or pretesting can also vary greatly in the amount of time and effort that is invested. Pretesting can be done on a small scale for curricula that will be implemented by a single extension trainer or subject matter expert. If a large scale training course is being designed, such as one for use in several different provinces of a country, then a more sophisticated and in-depth pretest would be required.

Regardless of the methods used or size and importance of curriculum, the tryout or pretesting should be systematically planned and implemented. The following section provides guidance in the design of a pretest for a curriculum.

Development Of a Plan For Tryout

Planning the pretest is as important as the planning of any worthwhile activity. If properly planned, the likelihood of the pretest in accomplishing its objective is greatly improved. The plan can be used as a guide or road map in the implementation of the pretest and can also facilitate the use of pretest results in improving the curriculum. The planning process involves the consideration of three basic steps. Each of these steps is outlined in the following paragraphs.

Determine The Purpose Of The Tryout

The purpose of pretesting a curriculum should be concisely stated in writing. This purpose statement should spell out the reason for doing the pretesting. It becomes the driving force for doing the pretest and assumes a role similar to a goal or objective. By putting the purpose statement in writing helps to communicate the reason for doing the pretest to all involved, and may alleviate any misconceptions or fears that are sometime associated with evaluations. An example purpose statement for pretesting follows.

DEVELOPMENT OF A PLAN FOR TRYOUT

Sample Purpose Statement for Pretesting

The purpose for the pretesting of the pesticide application course is to provide feedback to the developers so that they can revise the curriculum before it is implemented in the region.

Formulate Key Questions For The Pretesting

Key questions are major or important questions that identify things that the trainer, curriculum developer or training sponsor is concerned about. The questions are answered by the tryout. The selection of information and the collection of data are guided by the key questions. The following are example key questions.

Sample Key Questions for a Pretest

1. Are the objectives of the course appropriate for the intended participants?

2. Is the content of the course technically accurate?

3. Is the organization of the content optimal?

4 Are the best methods of instruction being used in each of the lessons?

Key questions are formulated by first identifying who has a stake in the pretest. If the extension trainer is the primary stakeholder and is most knowledgeable about the training needs, then this person should generate the key questions. If government level officials are supporting the design and implementation of the curriculum, then they should be interviewed to determine their interests and needs for the tryout. Based on this input, a set of questions should be developed.

After the questions are developed, they should be submitted to the important stakeholders or those supporting the training. They should have the opportunity to critique the questions and either approve them or make suggestions for change.

Identify Needed Information And Select Pretest Methods

Once key questions for the tryout are formulated and agreed upon, the next step is to determine how the questions can best be answered. This involves two interrelated steps. The first step is to identify the types of information that are important to answering the questions and then to determine where such information can be found. Many times, the questions lead you directly to the information while at other times a great deal of thought is necessary. The first sample key question posed before: 1. Are the objectives of the course appropriate for the intended participants? is fairly simple to interpret. This question is concerned with the appropriateness or relevance of course objectives. The question includes reference to participants, so the participants would be a primary source of information for answering this question. Also, you can logically think about the question and ask yourself " Whom could provide input to answering this question?" A response related to the first sample key question might be:

- Subject matter experts
- Local extension personnel
- Potential course participants.

After a list of information sources has been developed for each key question, the next step is to determine an appropriate method or technique for collecting the needed information. The pretesting of a curriculum as its name implies involves the tryout of the curriculum in some limited way before it is finalised or fully implemented. During the tryout, it is important to gather information and feedback from selected individuals. These individuals are those who have the best view of the curriculum during the pretesting. The following several paragraphs present a description of the most prominent methods used in the pretesting of training curricula.

Instructor Feedback

Instructors or trainers who are involved in the tryout of the curriculum are in the best position to judge its effectiveness and efficiency. These individuals must fully understand the instructions and content included in the curriculum. Additionally, these individuals must also have the technical or subject matter expertise to present and manage the content of the curriculum. The best way to collect instructor feedback during a pretest of a curriculum is to use a checklist or rating scale. Such an instrument can be used periodically throughout the tryout process and at the end of the course. A checklist or rating instrument allows for the collection of information from the instructor regarding what appears to be effective and what may have problems.

Instructors can also be asked to identify ways in which the curriculum can be improved. This can be accomplished through one of several potential approaches. The first involves the addition of questions on the checklist or rating scale that ask the instructor to make suggestions for revising the curriculum. A second approach involves the interview of the instructor(s) upon completion of tryout. These interviews can include specific questions related to needs and suggestions for improving the curriculum. This last approach becomes a debriefing session that is focused on improving the curriculum.

Student Feedback

The students or recipients of the training in the tryout phase are in an excellent position to provide feedback on the curriculum. Students can respond to specific rating scales that ask them to judge elements of the curriculum such as objectives, content, methods, evaluation procedures, and so on. Additionally, students can judge the quality of instruction that was used within the curriculum. Both of these types of judgements can lead to improvements in the curriculum.

Many training courses include an evaluation at the end of the course to provide feedback to the instructor on how well they thought the course was presented and to give an overall indication of how they liked the course. Evaluations such as these are useful to instructors and curriculum developers. However, in a pretesting situation, this type of evaluation can be expanded to provide more detailed information to the curriculum developer more often. For example, an instructor might ask the students to complete an evaluation form at the end of each unit, lesson or major component of the course. When students know the course is being offered for the first time or being pretested, they will usually be very cooperative in providing these additional evaluations.

Summaries of student feedback can be used by the curriculum developer to make changes in form and content of the course so that it works more effectively the next time it is taught or delivered.

Expert Feedback

Subject matter experts can be asked to review a curriculum and to provide feedback regarding the design and content of the curriculum. Additionally, curriculum development specialists can review the curriculum and

provide feedback about the form of objectives, design of lessons, selection of instructional methods, appropriateness of evaluation techniques, and other design related elements. Both of these types of expert review can be useful in improving the curriculum.

If expert review is used in pretesting a document, the process of review should be guided by a questionnaire or checklist that focuses the expert on the elements of the curriculum you are concerned with. The key questions that have been developed for the pretesting will dictate the content of the questionnaire.

Identifying experts to review a curriculum need not be a difficult task. A first step in identifying experts is to determine what type of expertise is important to the curriculum. Often, an expert is a colleague or co-worker of the curriculum developer. An extension subject matter specialist, an extension trainer, a local business director, may all be potential experts for review of the curriculum. Once identified, these selected experts should be contacted and asked to review the curriculum materials and to complete the questionnaire that has been designed. When they agree to help, they should be given the materials, instruments, and instructions for completing the review task.

In many cases, experts are debriefed in person by the curriculum developer following the review of the curriculum. This one-to-one relationship allows the curriculum developer to probe into the reasons why the expert made the judgements he or she has made. Also, this allows the curriculum developer to solicit ideas for improving the curriculum.

Expert review in pretesting can be done on a small or large scale basis. For example, a curriculum being developed by an extension trainer in Indonesia, may involve expert review by two people from the same extension unit or office. In another example, a curriculum developer may be evaluating a new curriculum for use in an entire region.

IMPLEMENT THE CURRICULUM

SECTION II / DEVELOPING CURRICULUM

This may necessitate the expert review of the curriculum by fifty people in several different countries. The magnitude of the curriculum and the resources available for pretesting will contribute to the decision on the scale of the pretest.

The plan for pretesting should include an indication of which methods will be used in the pretest. The selection should be based on which method or methods will be the most effective in collecting the information that is needed to answer the key questions. When feasible, more than one method should be used. This will provide a broader view of the curriculum and the developer will have more confidence in the results and in the suggestions for improvement.

Implement The Curriculum On a Tryout Basis

The implementation of the curriculum on a small scale basis is an ideal form of pretesting. It allows for the collection of information from the instructor(s) and from students. It provides a realistic test of how the curriculum will work when implemented on a broader scale. The small scale implementation should also allow the instructor and curriculum developer to make adjustment during the implementation process to smoothen the overall process. The following general procedures are suggested.

STEP 1.

Identify a time and place for the tryout

A time and place should be selected that meets the needs of the trainer and of the trainees or participants.
A location should be selected that is identical or similar to the place where the actual course will take place when fully implemented.

STEP 2.

Select and invite a small group of participants for the tryout

A group of participants should be selected to participate in the tryout. These participants should have the same general characteristics as the intended participants for the course. For example, if the course is designed for rice farmers who farm less than 3 hectares, then the tryout participants should come from the same group.

STEP 3.

Begin the course and proceed through the curriculum as designed

The course should be implemented as it was designed. This means that the lesson plans and other guides should be closely followed. Additionally, the support materials that have been designed for the course should also be used. Some adjustments may be necessary within the course due to uniqueness of the setting. However, any changes or adjustments should be noted by the instructor. A daily log kept by the instructor can be a useful means for keeping track of changes that were made.

STEP 4.

Collect feedback from participants at the end of major lessons or units of instruction

A feedback instrument should be prepared to elicit feedback from participants. This form or instrument can be general enough for use at the completion of every lesson or unit, or it can be customised to focus on a specific unit. Some units that have heavy field work may need special items that pertain to field work. The participants should be informed of the importance of their feedback to the revision of the curriculum and they should be asked to take them very seriously.

STEP 5.

Collect feedback from the instructor at the end of each major segment of instruction

The instructor should also document his or her reactions at the end of each major segment of instruction. This can be done by completing an instructor feedback form or by recording judgements in a daily log. If a daily log is used, every unit should include attention to 1) strengths of the unit, 2) weaknesses of the unit, and 3) suggestions for changing the unit.

STEP 6.

Collect information from participants and the instructor at the end of the course

At the end of the course, a global or broad instrument should be used to collect information from participants regarding the course. The same types of questions can be used at this point as were used at the end of each unit or lesson, except the focus should be on the course in total. Additional items regarding the facilities and other general elements may be added.

FORMULATE RECCOMANDATIONS

SECTION II / DEVELOPING CURRICULUM

Summarise Data And Formulate Recommendations

Following the implementation of the tryout, the information that has been collected should be summarised. The summary should include the participants responses at the end of each major block of instruction, the participant rating of the overall course, the instructor comments on each unit or lesson, the log of the instructor, and the end of course rating by the instructor. If the curriculum has been submitted to experts for review, their reactions should also be summarised.

The summaries should be organised around the key questions that were formulated as part of the pretesting plan. This can be done by taking each key question and sorting all the ratings and comments that pertain to it into one section. The following example talies one question.

Sample Summary of Results

Are the objectives of the course appropriate for the intended participants?

Participant lesson form item 2. Are the objectives appropriate to you?
   Yes 91% No 9%
Instructor lesson form item 4. Were objectives appropriate for the audience?
   Yes 100% No 0%
Expert feedback
One expert thought the objectives for lesson two involved knowledge that was not needed by rice farmers.

Once the results are summarised and categorised, the curriculum developer should review the summaries for each key question and ask himself or herself the question: "What does this mean for the curriculum?" The answers to this question should be conclusions about the curriculum. For example, after reviewing the sample results presented above a logical conclusion might be:

Sample Conclusion

Participants and instructors think the objectives of the course are appropriate. The objectives of lesson two were questioned by one expert.

Once conclusions are drawn, recommendations for changing the curriculum should be formulated. Where results indicate no problem, a recommendation is not needed. However, where conclusions indicate that something is deficient or inappropriate, a recommendation for change should be written. The recommendation tells the curriculum developer what to do to make the course better. A sample recommendation follows.

Sample Recommendation

Do not change the objectives of the course with the exception of unit 2. For unit 2, have to two additional experts react to the objectives and then revise based on their suggestions.

SUMMARY

SECTION II / DEVELOPING CURRICULUM

Make Changes In The Curriculum As Recommended

This final action involves reading the recommendations and taking action to implement them. If the recommendations are specific, then changes and revisions will be straight forward. If some recommendations are vague, they may need discussion or clarification prior to implementation. If properly done, the pretesting can result in an improved curriculum in which all the important stakeholders can have confidence. The ultimate test of the pretesting is in seeing if its original purpose has been achieved.

Summary

The tryout and pretesting of a curriculum is an important step in the curriculum development process. It ensures that the curriculum will work and it provides numerous opportunities for input and suggestions on how to improve the curriculum.

A plan for the pretesting is important to ensure that the pretesting is systematic and complete. The plan should include a purpose statement, a set of key questions and a list of methods that will be used in the pretest.

Implementation of the pretest typically involves tryout of the course on a small scale with collection of information from participants and instructors. However, expert feedback is also an important form of pretesting.

Additional References

Brandt, Ronald S. (1981)
Applied Strategies for curriculum evaluation.
Alexandria, Virginia: Association for Supervision and Curriculum Development.

Finch, Curtis R., & Cunkilton, John R. (1984)
Curriculum Development in Vocational and Technical Education: Planning, Content, and Implementation.
London : Allyn and Bacon, Inc.

Lawson, Tom E. (1974)
Formative Instructional Product Evaluation.
Englewood Cliffs, New Jersey: Educational Technology Publications.

Miller, Wilbur R. (1990)
Instructors and Their Jobs.
Homewood, Illinois : American Technical Publishers, Inc.

Wentling, Tim L. (1980)
Evaluating Occupational Education and Training Programs.
Urbana, Illinois: Griffon Press International

SECTION III

EXAMPLES OF TRAINING CURRICULA

Training curriculum
Example 1

EXAMPLE 1

Training curriculum
Example 1

NOTE

TRAINING CURRICULUM / EXAMPLE 1

NOTE

This example is presented to show the reader what a curriculum looks like. It is not presented to be an exceptional one. Rather, it shows what can be included and how specific items can be presented. A curriculum should be prepared in a form that is most useable by the trainers. Therefore, curriculum developers should be free to adapt and design their own format for curricula.

Course Title:

Group Discussion Methods in Integrated Pest Management (IPM) Training
(adapted from Training Module 4 of the Field-based Core Curriculum for IPM Extension Training Programme, FAO, 1988)

Purpose:

The course is designed to enable extension agents and trainers to use various group discussion methods in the delivery of IPM training. This course, taken in conjunction with the other IPM training courses, will help trainers to effectively communicate the importance of IPM and the methods by which IPM may be carried out. The implementation of IPM will eventually reduce the need for and risks associated with the concentrated use of chemical pesticides, while enabling farmers to maintain effective control of pests.

Course Objectives:

❶ To introduce to the trainees the purposes and instructional uses of various group discussion techniques.

❷ To enable the trainees to choose the appropriate techniques when conducting group discussions.

❸ To train the trainees to conduct group discussions using various techniques.

Training Methods and Techniques

❶ Classroom lectures

❷ Groupwork and discussions

❸ Field visit

❹ Assigned reading

Intended Audience:

The course is intended for extension agents and others responsible for providing IPM training to farmers in Vietnam.

Venue:

The course will be held at the Farmers Extension Training Centre at Nam Pen.

Logistical Arrangements:

Meals and accommodation will be at the centre's dormitory. Participants' daily allowance and travel expenses to the Centre will be borne by the Ministry of Agriculture.

Duration and Schedule:

The course will begin on 5 September 1994, at 8:00 and end on 8 September 1994 at 12:00.

Trainers/Resource Persons:

The course will be taught by Dr. Wun Hung Lo, Professor of Technical Education, University of Cantho, and Mr. Nguyen Van Thiew, Rodent Specialist, Plant Protection Department, Ministry of Agriculture, Vietnam.

SUMMARY COURSE STRUCTURE

COURSE: Group discussion method in integrated pest management (IPM)

OBJECTIVES:
1. To introduce to the trainees the purposes and instructional uses of various group discussion techniques.
2. To enable the trainees to choose the appropriate techniques when conducting group discussions.
3. To train the trainees to conduct group discussions using various techniques.

ACTIVITY					SUB-ACTIVITY				
No.	Title	Objective	Time Class	Time Field	No.	Title	Objective	Time Class	Time Field
1.1	The group discussion method	After this activity, the trainees will be able to explain the various techniques used in a group discussion that achieves a given objective	2h/15'		1.1.1.	The definition, purpose and use of group discussion	To define and describe the purpose of conducting group discussion and how to do it	45 min	
					1.2.1.	Procedure for conducting a group discussion	To discuss the procedure of a group discussion technique and to complete its given topic	1h	
						EVALUATION 1.1		30 min	
1.2	The brainstorming technique	After this activity, the trainees will be able, given a topic and situation, to use the brainstorming technique to generate a list of ideas relevant to the topic, rank them and select the most appropriate to the specific topic and situation	2h/45'		1.2.1.	The purpose and stages of brainstorming technique	To state the purpose of brainstorming, identify the situation when it can best be used, and the stages of the technique	45 min	
					1.2.2.	Preparing and conducting a brainstorming session	To list the important steps in preparing and conducting a brainstorming session.	30 min	

SUMMARY COURSE STRUCTURE

TRAINING CURRICULUM / EXAMPLE 1

ACTIVITY					SUB-ACTIVITY			
No.	Title	Objective	Time Class	Field	No.	Title	Objective	Time Class / Field
1.2					1.2.3.	Brainstorming	Given a specific topic, to conduct a brainstorming activity that achieves the task of generating, ranking and selecting ideas appropriate to the topic	1h
						EVALUATION 1.2		
1.3	The critical incident	After this activity, the trainees will be able to use the critical incident to start a discussion on a given topic.	1h/20'		1.3.1.	The purpose and use of the critical incident	To describe the critical incident, its purpose and use	40min
					1.3.2.	How to use the critical incident	To explain all the requirements and preparation needed and how the critical incident is used	20 min
						EVALUATION 1.3		20 min
1.4	The picture starter	After this activity, the trainees will be able to readily adapt and use the picture starter method for their farmers training	2h/20'		1.4.1.	The purpose of the picture starter	To describe the purpose of the picture starter method	20min
					1.4.2.	How to conduct a picture starter sessionn	To list all the steps needed in conducting a picture starter session	1h

SUMMARY COURSE STRUCTURE

SECTION III / EXAMPLES OF TRAINING CURRICULA

ACTIVITY					SUB-ACTIVITY				
No.	Title	Objective	Time Class	Time Field	No.	Title	Objective	Time Class	Time Field
1.4					1.4.3.	Using the picture starter	To use the picture starter to get farmers focus their thinking and talk about their experience on the major pests in their fields	40min	
						EVALUATION 1.4		20min	
1.5	The buzz session	After this activity, the trainees will be able to conduct buzz session in order to generate intense discussion on a controversial topic within short time	1h/45'		1.5.1.	What is a buzz session?	To explain what is a buzz session	20min	
					1.5.2.	How to conduct a buzz session	To list all the steps in conducting a buzz session	45min	
					1.5.3.	Using the buzz session	To use a buzz session to generate intense discussion and get lots of ideas on a given topic within a short time	20min	
						EVALUATION 1.5		20min	
1.6	Scaring session	Upon completion of this activity, the trainees will be able to conduct a scaring session according to a given objective	2h/20'	2 h	1.6.1.	Definition and purpose of a scaring session	To define what is a scaring session and its purpose	20min	
					1.6.2.	Organising a scaring session	To organise a scaring session according to specific objectives	30min	

TRAINING CURRICULUM / EXAMPLE 1

ACTIVITY					SUB-ACTIVITY			
No.	Title	Objective	Time Class	Time Field	No.	Title	Objective	Time Class	Time Field
1.6					1.6.3.	Conducting a scaring session to motivate farmers to practice IPM	To prepare and conduct a scaring session that will motivate farmers to practice IPM	1h	2h
						EVALUATION 1.6		30min	
1.7	Role playing	After the acitivity, the trainees will be able to write and conduct a role playing according to a given instruction objective	2h/30'		1.7.1.	The role playing methos	To describe th role playing method, its purpose, uses, and the process of a role playing activiy	1h	
					1.7.2.	Conducting a role playing	Given a topic, to design and conduct a role playing	2h	
					1.7.3.	EVALUATION 1.7		30min	

	CLASS	FIELD	TOTAL
TOTAL INSTRUCTIONAL HOURS FOR COURSE	15H/15'	2H	17H/15'

SECTION III / EXAMPLES OF TRAINING CURRICULA

> **NOTE**
>
> The remaining pages of this example provide the detailed components of Activity 1.1: The Group Discussion. Though they are not presented in this example, similar detailed components would exist in the curriculum's for Activities 1.2 to 1.6 (Brainstorming, Critical Incident, Picture Starter, Buzz Session, Scaring Session, Role Playing).

ACTIVITY FACE SHEET 1.1

Title :	The Group Discussion Method
Objectives :	After this activity, the trainees will be able to explain the various techniques used in a group discussion that achieves a given objective
Sub-Activity:	**1.1.1** The definition, purpose and use of group discussion **1.1.2** Procedure for conducting a group discussion Evaluation 1.1
Time:	2 hours 15 minutes
Materials needed:	Blackboard and chalks; Newsprints and felt pens; Handouts 1.1.1/1.1.2; Evaluation Sheet 1.1
Location:	Classroom
Preparation and set-up procedures:	Three days before the activity: prepare the needed materials and reproduce the handouts and the Evaluation form.
Cross references and suggested reading materials	All the group discussions that were conducted during the previous activities. A.W. Van den Ban, and H.S. Hawkins, 1988: "Agricultural extension", Longman Scientific & Tech. p. 153 - 164.

ACTIVITY 1.1   TRAINING CURRICULUM / EXAMPLE 1

ACTIVITY 1.1

Title :	The Group Discussion Method
Objectives :	After this activity, the trainees will be able to explain the various techniques used in a group discussion that achieves a given objective
Time:	2 hours 15 minutes

CONTENTS AND INSTRUCTION	METHODS AND MATERIALS
Trainers instruction This activity will be conducted in the classroom. Its purpose is to give the trainees an opportunity to analyse the group discussion as an extension method. They have already experienced this method for several times, but now they will practice it to analyse its value as an extension method, to take action or decision for the extensioin programme. **Introduction** We start now with group discussion the analysis of several extension methods that you will use for your farmers' training. This is a useful method because it requires the participation of all the trainees and allows an effective exchange of information and experience among them. You have already tried it in former activities, so please recall those experiences in this case.	 Oral presentation

SUB-ACTIVITY 1.1.1

Title : The Definition, Purpose and Use of Group Discussion

Objectives : To define and describe the purpose of conducting group discussion and how to do it

Time: 45 minutes

CONTENTS AND INSTRUCTION	METHODS AND MATERIALS
Trainer's instruction	
The purpose of this sub-activity is to conduct group discussion to provide the participants with a basis for discussing this extension method and to provide you with a practical reference for the following briefing. Write the topic for discussion on the board. After the discussion starts, you can help with the more specific questions. Write these questions on the board under the main topic.	Chalkboard or whiteboard
We will now do a group discussion to understand better this method in all its parts. Please sit in a circle, so all of you can see each other. The topic to discuss for the next half an hour is:	Group discussion
"What is the meaning of IPM?"	
I would like one of you to write on the board the important ideas that come out of the discussion. I will help you by identifying and summarising them. We can break	

CONTENTS AND INSTRUCTION	METHODS AND MATERIALS
down the main topic in more specific questions:	
"What does IPM teach farmers?"	Chalkboard or whiteboard
"What do we want farmers to be able to do after the IPM training?"	
"What differences can farmers expect in their lives or economic well-being if they practice IPM and why?"	
Those questions will lead you to explain better the main topic: you see how close you come to answering the first question. They serve to give more structure to the discussion.	
Trainer's instruction	
After actually conducting the group discussion, summarise its conclusions and give a briefing referring to that actual experience.	
The group discussion method is a meeting for discussing a topic of mutual interest. The discussion is coordinated by a group leader/facilitator, who however should never prevail in the discussion, but only give directions for its smooth flow. The topic for discussion can be assigned by the discussion leader/facilitator or by the group itself.	**Briefing**

CONTENTS AND INSTRUCTION	METHODS AND MATERIALS
Group discussions are most effective with 6 to 8 people, but up to 20 people can take part. Small groups encourage more sharing. Large groups are often dominated by those who are outgoing. Shy people get lost in a large group. So you may consider the possibility of dividing a large group into small groups to discuss a topic. The purpose of holding a group discussion is to examine and reflect on a topic of importance to the group members, to state and solve common problems. All of the members of the group should give their contribution. This sharing of ideas on a subject helps each member to understand how others perceive and think about a subject. It also offers an opportunity to learn from others. As we did before, the position of the group in a circle facilitate the members in the communication process. Good discussions must have a focus and structure to be productive. These can be provided by a good group leader/facilitator, who introduces a topic that is clearly stated, and follows an agenda keeping the discussion within the trace using appropriate specific questions. In the former case, I was acting as a facilitator, the goal was stated in the first questions, and the following questions were giving a trace to come to a logical definition of the meaning of IPM.	

SUB-ACTIVITY 1.1.1   **TRAINING CURRICULUM / EXAMPLE 1**

CONTENTS AND INSTRUCTION	METHODS AND MATERIALS
The group discussion can be used in several ways. As an educational method it allows members to see and hear a subject from several points of view. In fact you see the different points of views you expressed about IPM. Usually group members are asked to prepare some background information to share during the group discussion. This does not mean reading only. In IPM you share information you acquired through field experience. Farmers could be asked to try a new skill that you have taught them, and then they can discuss about it. Generally group discussion is conducted for problem solving. In this case it aims to examine a problem and get different viewpoints on it. The value of these varied opinions in finding appropriate solutions is that something may come up as a creative and effective solution that an individual would not think of on his own. A group discussion can enhance knowledge as it broadens the group's understanding on a subject. Also group discussion can be used to influence attitudes and to motivate people.	

CONTENTS AND INSTRUCTION	METHODS AND MATERIALS
The advantages of group discussion are: ■ the opportunity for members to learn from each other rather than just from experts; ■ it can be readily combined with other activities; and it helps in consolidating the ideas generated during these activities; ■ it encourages active listening and participation as members react to and think about each other's statements. **The limitations of this method are:** ■ the participants can lose their focus; the group facilitator should then pay attention to keep them on the subject; ■ some of the members may dominate the discussion; ■ there is need for some back ground knowledge on the topic, for the discussion to be useful; ■ the group should be homogeneous and not too large. *Trainer's instruction* *Distribute the handout and close the session.*	 Handout 1.1.1 - The definition, purpose and use of group discussion

SUB-ACTIVITY 1.1.2

Title :	Procedure for Conducting a Group Discussion
Objectives :	To discuss the procedure of a group discussion and to complete its given topic
Time:	1 hour

CONTENTS AND INSTRUCTION	METHODS AND MATERIALS
Trainer's instruction	
You will start with a briefing, to present more details on the procedure of a group discussion technique. While talking, write the underlined words on the board, and refer to what happened in the former group discussion for all the stages.	Chalkboard/or whiteboard
The purpose of the group discussion is:	**Briefing**
a to solve a problem;	
b to explore an issue;	
c to plan an activity.	
In any case, it goes through several stages:	
1 All participants need to clearly **understand** the topic under discussion. This should be stated at the beginning by the facilitator who is also in charge of maintaining the discussion within its trace.	

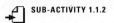

SECTION III / EXAMPLES OF TRAINING CURRICULA

CONTENTS AND INSTRUCTION	METHODS AND MATERIALS
❷ Members begin to react to the topic by offering ideas. There may be opposing ideas, being this the ideal condition for the development of an useful discussion. The facilitator's task is to avoid bitterness among participants for this reason. ❸ Members begin to test ideas or solutions by comparing them to what they know; ideas are analysed and problems defined. ❹ When ideas are found to be in conflict with the facts, they are revised or discarded. Selection is made among ideas and solutions. ❺ The revised and selected ideas are tested against what members know to be true. The final answer or solution is defined by the group, with the assistance of the facilitator. We might suggest some points for the facilitator to remember: ⓐ Create a feeling of confidence in the group by: ■ calling a homogeneous group, to avoid conflicts; ■ begin with an introduction of the group members; ■ avoiding dominant people to prevail, stimulating others' intervention;	

CONTENTS AND INSTRUCTION	METHODS AND MATERIALS
• using participants' words and writing them on the board; this will reward and encourage them in the discussion. **b)** Stimulate interest in the topic by: • clearly stating the topic, possibly in a question form written on the board; • causing participants' reaction to the given topic; • summarising ideas offered by the participants. **c)** Encourage participation by: • politely interrupting those dominating; • asking questions to those not participating; • encouraging members to discuss among each other; • keeping discussion focused on topic, through more specific questions leading to the main goal. **d)** Examine and integrate statements and ideas by: • restating ideas suggested and asking for further reaction;	

CONTENTS AND INSTRUCTION	METHODS AND MATERIALS
■ asking for others' supporting or opposing ideas; ■ summarising on the board the important ideas. **e** Maintain interest by: ■ encouraging trust and good humour; ■ relating discussion to familiar things; ■ helping members to see how the discussion is progressing towards the goal initially stated; ■ providing breaks if necessary. **f** Close discussion by: ■ summarising important points and agreements reached; ■ comparing results with goals to see what needs to be done as a follow-up to this meeting, and getting commitment for action; ■ thanking participants for their useful contribution.	 Handout 1.1.2 - Procedure for conducting a group discussion
Trainer's instruction *Now divide them into groups fo 5-6. Give each group newsprints and felt pens for reports. Write the topic on the board, and give the following instruction:*	Newsprint and felt pens

SUB-ACTIVITY 1.1.2

TRAINING CURRICULUM / EXAMPLE 1

CONTENTS AND INSTRUCTION	METHODS AND MATERIALS
"How can chemical sales people be involved in helping farmers learn IPM skills?" Now please ask each group to discuss this topic, and get to an answer. One leader for each group and one person to report on: **a** Answer **b** How the discussion proceeded within the group, good and bad points. In order to structure your discussion towards the final goal you might consider these more specific questions: "Why should chemical dealers be interested in helping farmers learn IPM skills?" "Is there any way in which chemical dealers can benefit from farmers practising IPM?" Please formulate other specific questions and report them with their answers. Discuss for 30 minutes, then report for 10 minutes. I will circulate among the working groups and see how the discussion proceeds. *Trainer's instruction* *After 30 minutes have the reports presented, ask for comments and questions. Finally ask:*	**Exercise** Small groups discussion

CONTENTS AND INSTRUCTION	METHODS AND MATERIALS
"How do you think group discussion method will be useful in you IPM extension programme?"	Group discussion
Trainer's instruction	
Distribute the Evaluation form to each trainee, and have them answer the questions. Collect the forms after 30 minutes and read them, pointing out unclear topics for your trainees. You will review these topics with them BEFORE starting the next activity.	Evaluation form 1.1

HANDOUT 1.1.1   TRAINING CURRICULUM / EXAMPLE 1

THE DEFINITION, PURPOSE AND USE OF GROUP DISCUSSION METHOD

The group discussion method is a meeting for discussing a topic of mutual interest. The discussion is coordinated by a group leader/facilitator, who however should never prevail in the discussion, but only give directions for its smooth flow. The topic for discussion can be assigned by the discussion leader/facilitator or by the group itself.

Group discussions are most effective with 6 to 8 people, but up to 20 people could take part. Small groups encourage more sharing. Large groups are often dominated by those who are outgoing. Shy people get lost in a large group. So you may consider the possibility of dividing a large group into small groups to discuss a topic.

The purpose in holding a group discussion is to examine and reflect on a topic of importance to the group members, to state and solve common problems. All of the members of the group should give their contribution. This sharing of ideas on a subject helps each member to understand how others perceive and think about a subject. It also offers an opportunity to learn from others. As we did before, the position of the group in a circle facilitate the members in the communication process.

Good discussions must have a focus and structure to be productive. These can be provided by a good group leader/facilitator, who introduces a topic that is clearly stated, and follows an agenda keeping the discussion within the trace using appropriate specific questions. In the former case, I was acting as a facilitator, the goal was stated in the first questions, and the following questions were giving a trace to come to a logical definition of the meaning of IPM.

The group discussion can be used in several ways. As an educational method it allows members to see and hear a subject from several points of view. In fact you see the different points of views you expressed about IPM. Usually group members are asked to prepare some background information to share during the group discussion. This does not mean reading only. In IPM you share information you acquired through field experience. Farmers could be asked to try a new skill that you have taught them, and then they can discuss about it.

Generally group discussion is conducted for problem solving. In this case it aims to examine a problem and get different viewpoints on it. The value of these varied opinions in finding appropriate solutions is that something may come up as a creative and effective solution that an individual would not think of on his own.

A group discussion can enhance knowledge as it broadens the group's understanding on a subject. Also group discussion can be used to influence attitudes and to motivate people.

The advantages of group discussion are:

- the opportunity for members to learn from each other rather than just from experts;
- it can be readily combined with other activities; and it helps in consolidating the ideas generated during these activities;
- it encourages active listening and participation as members react to and think about each other's statements.

The limitations of this method are:

- the participants can lose their focus; the group facilitator should then pay attention to keep them on the subject;
- some of the members may dominate the discussion;
- there is need for some background knowledge on the topic, for the discussion to be useful;
- the group should be homogeneous and not too large.

PROCEDURE FOR CONDUCTING A GROUP DISCUSSION

The purpose of the group discussion is:

a to solve a problem;

b to explore an issue;

c to plan an activity

In any case, it goes through several stages:

1 All participants need to clearly understand the topic under discussion. This should be stated at the beginning by the facilitator who is also in charge of maintaining the discussion within its trace.

2 Members begin to react to the topic by offering ideas. There may be opposing ideas, being this the ideal condition for the development of an useful discussion. The facilitator's task is to avoid bitterness among participants for this reason.

3 Members begin to test ideas or solutions by comparing them to what they know; ideas are analysed and problems defined.

4 When ideas are found to be in conflict with the facts, they are revised or discarded. Selection is made among ideas and solutions.

5 The revised and selected ideas are tested against what members know to be true. The final answer or solution is defined by the group, with the assistance of the facilitator.

We might suggest some points for the facilitator to remember:

a Create a feeling of confidence in the group by:

- calling a homogeneous group, to avoid conflicts;
- begin with an introduction of the group members;

- avoiding dominant people to prevail, stimulating others' intervention;
- using participants' words and writing them on the board; this will reward and encourage them in the discussion.

b Stimulate interest in the topic by:
- clearly stating the topic, possibly in a question form written on the board;
- causing participants' reaction to the given topic;
- summarising ideas offered by the participants.

c Encourage participation by:
- politely interrupting those dominating;
- asking questions to those not participating;
- encouraging members to discuss among each other;
- keeping discussion focused on topic, through more specific questions leading to the main goal.

d Examine and integrate statements and ideas by:
- restating ideas suggested and asking for further reaction;
- asking for others' supporting or opposing ideas;
- summarising on the board the important ideas.

e Maintain interest by:
- encouraging trust and good humour;
- relating discussion to familiar things;
- helping members to see how the discussion is

- progressing towards goals initially stated;
- providing breaks if necessary.

❶ Close discussion by:

- summarising important points and agreements reached;
- comparing results with goals to see what needs to be done as a follow-up to this meeting, and getting commitment action;
- thanking participants for their useful contribution.

EVALUATION FORM 1.1

Name .... Date .... Place ....

PLEASE REFER TO THE CONTENT OF THIS ACTIVITY AND ANSWER THE FOLLOWING QUESTIONS: (30 minutes)

What is the ideal number of people for a group discussion?

What are the advantages and disadvantages of group discussion as an extension method?

What is the role of the facilitator?

Please list the stages that a group discussion usually goes through:

Please name one way to begin discussion to get participation from group members:

What should you do in closing a discussion?

You should never summarise the main points during the discussion, only at the end: true or false?

Training curriculum
Example 2

EXAMPLE 2

Training curriculum Example 2

TRAINING CURRICULUM / EXAMPLE 2

NOTE

This example is presented to show the reader what a curriculum looks like. It is not presented to be an exceptional one. Rather, it shows what can be included and how specific items can be presented. A curriculum should be prepared in a form that is most useable by the trainers. Therefore, curriculum developers should be free to adapt and design their own format for curricula.

Course Title:

Establishing and Tending Softwood Plantations
(adapted from Tech. Forestry Education, FAO Industry Paper 47, 1984; and the Forestry Management Unit, Illinois Agricultural Core Curriculum Revision, University of Illinois, 1990)

Purpose:

The course is intended to augment the technical knowledge base of forest technicians. A forest technician is the link between forestry professionals and researchers and manual, or day-to-day forestry workers. Forestry technicians must possess a broad range of technical knowledge skills to adequately provide this link. This course provides one aspect of these necessary technical knowledge and skill areas.

Course Objective:

To develop the trainees' capabilities to establish and tend Softwood Plantations.

Training Methods and Techniques:

1. Classroom lectures
2. Groupwork and discussions
3. Field visit
4. Demonstration

Intended Audience:

The course is intended for all prospective forest technicians in _____ , and for those employed as forest technicians who need to update their plantation skills.

Venue:

The course will be held at the Forestry Department of _____ Technical College, _____ .

Logistical Arrangement:

Partecipans will be accomodated in the college residential hostel. Meals will be served at the Cafeteria. All costs are charged to the participants' sponsors.

Duration and Schedule:

The course will be held from 10 through 13 January 1994, with sessions beginning at 8:00 and ending at approximately 17:00 each day.

Trainers/Resource Person:

The resource person for the course is Mr. _____ , assistant professor of forestry, _____ Technical College, _____ .

SECTION III / EXAMPLES OF TRAINING CURRICULA

LESSON PLAN

Unit Title :	Establishing and Tending Softwood Plantations
Lesson Title :	Introduction to Plantations
Objectives :	On completion of this lesson, trainees will be able to:
	❶ Explain the reasons for the establishement of plantations based on standard practices
	❷ Select an appropriate site suitable for a softwood plantation
	❸ Name recommended species of softwood for the plantation

Topic	Method	Time	Resources
Introduction to plantations	Lecture	30 min	Holand, Rolfe, & Anderson
Factors in choosing a site	Lecture/ discussion	1 hour	Curriculum guide
Factors in a choosing species	Lecture/ discussion	2 hours	Curriculum guide

Practical/Field-Based Exercises :	Study the examples showing sites of softwood plantations
Practical Assignmment :	Given several written descriptions of sites and list of factors associated with each site, participants will choose an appropiate site for a softwood plantation
Evaluation Method :	Instructor will compare participant's site choice with the most correct choice

TRAINING CURRICULUM / EXAMPLE 2

LESSON PLAN

Course Title :	Establishing and Tending Softwood Plantations
Lesson Title :	Preparing a Site for Planting
Objectives :	On completion of this lesson, trainees will be able:
	❶ Clear plantation area suitable for ground preparation work
	❷ Prepare the ground ready for planting using mechanical method
	❸ Decide on the correct spacing for plantings based on recommendations

Topic	Method	Time	Resources
Controlling water, clearing various types of sites	Demonstration/ practice	4 hours	Site, site plans, tools
Ground preparation (hoeing, harrowing)	Demonstration/ practice	4 hours	Site, site ploughing, plans, tools
Factor affecting spacing of plantings	Lecture/ demonstration	2 hours	Curruculum site plans

Practical/Field-Based Exercises :	Operate clearing and ground prepartion machinery and/or equipemnt
Practical Assignmment :	Properly clear and prepare a sample site for planting

Evaluation Method :	Formative instructor evaluation of site preparation. Summative instructor evaluation of finished site

243

LESSON PLAN   SECTION III / EXAMPLES OF TRAINING CURRICULA

LESSON PLAN

Course Title :	Establishing and Tending Softwood Plantations
Lesson Title :	Planting Operations
Objectives :	On completion of this lesson, trainees will be able to:

    ❶ Follow proper procedures to transport and distribute softwood plants for planting

    ❷ State the appropriate time for softwood during establishment of plantation

    ❸ Check stock and determine number of surviving plants at planting site

    ❹ Demonstrate the use of pesticides and safety equiment for plant protection

Topic	Method	Time	Resources
Plant handling	Demonstration	1 hour	Plantings
Timing of plantings	Lecture/ discussion	1 hour	Curriculum guide
Stock checking/survivor counting	Demonstration	1 hour	Site, plantings
Using insecticides	Demonstration	1 hour	Site, plantings, insecticide, safety equipment

Practical/Field-Based Exercises :	Demonstrate various procedures for establishing and tending softwood plantation
Practical Assignmment :	Plant plantings on sample site
Evaluation Method :	Instructor evaluation of plant spacing and condition at finished sample site

LESSON PLAN

Course Title :	Establishing and Tending Softwood Plantations
Lesson Title :	Controlling Weeds
Objectives :	On completion of this lesson, trainees will be able to:
	❶ Identify different methods of weed control in newly established softwood plantation
	❷ Explain the selection criteria and select one or more weed control methods suitable for softwood plantation
	❸ Demotrate the safe handling and application of chemical pesticides to control weed

Topic	Method	Time	Resources
Methods of weed control	Lecture/ demonstration	3 hours	Curriculum guide, tools, pesticide labels
Selection criteria	Lecture/ discussion	1 hour	Curriculum guide,
Pesticide application	Demonstration/ practice	2 hours	Pesticide, safety equipment, application equipment
Mechanical weed control	Demontration/ practice	2 hours	Cultivation equipment

Practical/Field-Based Exercises :	Operation of pesticide spray equipment
Practical Assignmment :	Demonstrate proficiency in using weed control methods
Evaluation Method :	Instructor evaluation of performance on site

LESSON PLAN   SECTION III / EXAMPLES OF TRAINING CURRICULA

LESSON PLAN

Course Title :	Establishing and Tending Softwood Plantations
Lesson Title :	Pruning
Objectives :	On completion of this lesson, trainees will be able to: ❶ State reasons and importance for pruning softwood plants ❷ Discuss and explain two types/methods of pruning softwood ❸ Demonstrate a suitable pruning method for softwood using the pruning tools provided

Topic	Method	Time	Resources
Reasons for pruning	Lecture	1 hour	Curriculum guide
Types/methods of pruning	Demonstration	2 hours	Site, tools
Pruning practices	Practice	2 hours	Site, tools

Practical/Field-Based Exercises :	Practice pruning of softwood
Practical Assignmment :	Prune trees using appropiate methods
Evaluation Method :	Instructor inspection of pruned trees

LESSON PLAN   **TRAINING CURRICULUM** / EXAMPLE 2

LESSON PLAN

Course Title:	Establishing and Tending Softwood Plantations
Lesson Title:	Thinning
Objectives:	On completion of this lesson, trainees will be able to:
	❶ State clearly the purposes of thinning softwood plants in the plantation
	❷ Identify two most commonly used methods of thinning using the tools provided
	❸ Develop a comprehensive plan for thinning the plantation based on the rationale and the methods recommended

Topic	Method	Time	Resources
Purposes of thinning	Lecture	1 hour	Curriculum guide
Thinning methods	Lecture demonstration	2 hours	Curriculum guide site
Selection of thinnings	Demonstration	2 hours	Site
Felling trees for thinning	Demonstration	2 hours	Site, tools

Practical/Field-Based Exercises:	Survey field site for thinning
Practical Assignment:	Develop a thinning plan, including rationale and method
Evaluation Method:	A written thinning plan will be evaluated by instructor

INSTRUCTOR'S GUIDE

REFERENCES

❶ *

Forests and Forestry. Holand, Rolfe, Anderson. Interstate Publishers, Inc., P.O. Box 50, Danville, Il 61834-0050, (217) 446-0500.

❷ *

Agricultural Resources - Fish, Wildlife, Recreation, Forest Resource Management. Instructional Materials Service, F.E. Box 2588, Texas A & M University, College Station, TX 77843-2588.

❸

Various Materials. Instructional Materials Laboratory, 10 Industrial Education Building, University of Missouri-Columbia, Columbia, MO.

INSTRUCTOR'S NOTES AND REFERENCES

*
Indicates highly recommended reference

INFORMATION SHEET TRAINING CURRICULUM / EXAMPLE 2

SILVICULTURAL PRACTICES

Silviculture is the application of cutting practices to forest stands to increase their productivity.

Types of Silvicultural Cuttings

❶ Intermediate cuttings – Harvesting timber at any time from the reproduction stage to timer maturity. The principle objectives of intermediate cuttings are:

  ⓐ The improvement of the existing stand.

  ⓑ The regulation of tree and stand growth.

  ⓒ The opportunity for early financial returns.

  ⓓ Reduction of conditions favourable for forest pests.

  ⓔ The creation of conditions favourable to reproduction.

❷ Thinnings – A form of intermediate cutting in immature or young trees which improves the yield of the stand as a whole. The principle objectives of thinning are:

  ⓐ To regulate the distribution of growing space for the remaining trees.

  ⓑ To utilise to the best financial advantage all the merchant-able material produced by the stand during its rotation.

Various methods or techniques have been developed for thinning timber. Thinning methods include:

ⓐ Low thinning – Trim small short trees in the stand (trimming from below).

ⓑ Crown thinning – Remove the taller trees in the stand to open up the canopy (trimming from above).

ⓒ Selection thinning – The best trees in the stand are harvested.

❸ Cleaning – Method used to free the desired trees for competition from undesirable trees. Types of cleaning methods are as follows:

ⓐ Prescription burning – The use of fire under carefully controlled conditions is the most economical cleaning tool in young pines. Prescription burning is effective in controlling scrub hardwood up to four inches dbh on pine sites.

ⓑ Cutting – Cutting has limited use as a clearning method to do the labour involved.

ⓒ Basal spraying – The application of herbicides to all bark around the tree base. Basal spraying is a very selective and reliable method, but an expensive one for clearning.

ⓓ Foliage spraying – The spraying of hardwood foliage with herbicides is effective for broadcast control methods.

ⓔ Stenlants – Stenlants are gaining increasing popularity for sight treatments prior to planting. The chemicals generally persist in the soil for a year or more, so planting is delayed.

INFORMATION SHEET — **TRAINING CURRICULUM / EXAMPLE 2**

4 Liberation cuttings – A liberation cutting is one designed to free a young stand from competition from older trees. Overtopping is usually done to clear the canopy. There are several methods for controlling older, inferior trees:

- **a** Girdling – Involves cutting through the bark and cambium and into the sapwood with an axe or mechanical tool.

- **b** Basal spraying – The application of herbicide to the bark around the tree base.

5 Improvement cuttings – Done to improve the stands composition, quality and condition by removing inferior trees. Improvement cuttings are generally used in older stands that have not had the benefit of cleanings or liberation cuttings. Improvement cuttings should precede a harvest cut by a significant number of years. Types of improvement cuttings are:

- **a** Sanitation cuttings – A sanitation cutting is used to remove trees with insects or attracted by diseases.

- **b** Salvage cuttings – Much like sanitation cuttings except salvage cut trees have a salable value.

- **c** Pruning – The removal of side branches from trees to produce knot-free lumber from logs of higher quality.

6 Harvest cuttings – This silvicultural practice involves the removal of the mature timber, establishment of reproduction, and supplemental treatments of the timber-growing site. The methods of harvest cutting are as follows:

- **a** Clear cutting – In this method, virtually all the trees in the stand, both large and small, are cut.

- **b** Seed tree cutting – Seed tree cutting is a form of clear cutting, except that the seed-bearing trees are left suitably dispersed throughout the harvest area.

(c) Shelterwood cutting – Method in which only a portion of the stand is removed at any one time. Its purpose is to obtain natural reproduction under the partial shelter of a number of seed trees.

(d) Selection cutting – Complex method of cutting and removing individual trees throughout the stand based on maturity, growth rate, diameter and vigour.

INFORMATION SHEET **TRAINING CURRICULUM / EXAMPLE 2**

Tree Planting

Estimate needs – It is very important to order the proper number and species required for the area to be reforested.

Care of seedlings upon receiving from nursery – It is important that seedlings be planted as soon as possible upon receipt from the nursery. If planting must be delayed because of weather, the seedling bales should be opened and the trees heeled in at the planting site.

Tree spacing – The choice of spacing of pine trees is dependent upon the owner's objective. A spacing of 6 x 8 feet or 8 x 8 feet favours maximum cubic feet volume growth. A spacing of 8 x 12 feet is needed to permit passage of trucks or other equipment. Spacings of 10 x 10 feet or 12 x 12 feet may be used when trees of large diameter are desired in a relatively short time.

Planting procedure – As a rule, about 75 to 80 percent of all properly planted seedlings will survive. The three major methods of planting seedlings are hand planting, bar planting, and machine planting. Whether planting pine seedlings with a machine or by hand, there are certain procedures that must be followed:

❶ Plant the seedlings slightly lower, never higher, than it grows in the nursery.

❷ Plant seedlings in an upright position with the roots straight down.

❸ Always pack soil firmly around the roots to hold trees in an upright position.

❹ Plant only one tree in a given spot.

SECTION IV

APPENDICES

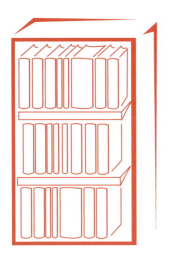

Glossary of terms

APPENDIX 1

audio-visual materials
Training support materials that are used to augment various training methods. These materials usually rely on seeing or hearing, but may also rely on other senses for input. Typical audio-visual materials include, photographs, video and audio tapes, posters, etc.

case study
A classroom training method that entails providing the students with information from real-life situations and directing them to solve problems associated with the situation. Case studies provide a way for instructors to see students apply theories, methods and procedures advanced in the course.

competency
Demonstrated ability (including knowledges, skills or attitudes) to perform a specific task successfully to meet a specified standard.

conditions
Anything called for as a requirement before the performance or completion of a job or task. The circumstances or restrictions imposed on a trainee when he or she is demonstrating a skill, engaged in a behaviour, or completing a task.

constructed response test items
Items which require a student to write or verbalise a response to a question. Examples of constructed response items include, short answer, definitions and essay questions.

criteria/criterion
A test by which a judgement of something can be formed. A performance standard or a specified statement on which a judgement or decision may be based (also called standard or performance level).

curriculum
The grand design or blueprint for training. The curriculum spells out the content to be covered in training, specifies the expectations for trainees, delineates procedures for covering content, suggests the methods for facilitating the learning process, identifies ways for evaluating or assessing learning, and puts everything in a time frame.

curriculum development
Is the process used to identify training needs, prepare training objectives, identify and organise training content, select methods for training, and developing support materials for training and trainee assessment.

demonstration
An illustrated lecture or a presentation that requires the instructor to carry out a process or series of actions so that trainees can observe and understand the procedure, principle or task.

evaluation
The process of using data collected by various forms of measurement or assessment to judge or make decisions about the merit or worth of an educational program or operation. A judgement of the worth or quality of an individual's performance.

field demonstrations
Demonstrations of varying length that are conducted in a real-life setting. These can take the form of observational visits all the way to hands on demonstrations with practitioners.

gap analysis
An integral step in determining training content needs. Gap analysis determines if training is an appropriate method for bridging the gap between desired performance and actual performance.

goals
A statement of broad general direction or intent. In an instructional setting, a goal may be a central purpose in teaching-learning or an overall terminal focus to be distinguished from an objective by having a greater breadth or scope.

group discussion
A verbal exchange of ideas, points of view, subject matter, and perceptions among trainer and the trainees for the purpose of clarifying or enriching understanding of the content being covered in the training activity.

job
The composite of duties and tasks performed regularly in one's trade, occupation or profession (i.e. job - duty - task - step).

job analysis
An integral step in determining training content needs. Job analysis involves the disassembly of a job or major work event into its component parts. It is a way of determining what is involved in a particular job.

lesson plan
Also called a training plan. The plan serves as a written record of how training will be conducted. The lesson plan is designed for the specific use of, and serves as a guide for the trainer. The plan usually will contain the following elements: objectives, content outline, training methods, time estimates, needed training resources, participant assignments and evaluation method.

measurement
A systematic, objective, procedure concerned with developing quantitative descriptions of a student's performance or behaviour.

needs analysis
A disciplined method of determining if present conditions require change. Needs analysis will assist in determining if the situation can be affected by training interventions, and if so, what specific topics, materials and methods may be most effective in bringing about the desired changes.

needs identification
The process of determining what deficits are present in the job or program. Needs Identification is a part of the needs analysis process where problems are defined and where potential solutions are listed. Both needs analysis and needs identification are integral parts of the curriculum development process.

objective
A specific aim, something to be striven for. In the context of training an objective is given in terms of specific trainee knowledge or skills that will be observed or measured at the end of training.

performance objectives
A statement, in measurable terms, of what behaviour the learner will be able to exhibit under specified conditions. Each performance objective is composed of three parts: performance, conditions and criterion or standard.

performance test
A type of measurement or test in which a skill or task is specified and the students are required to actually perform the task using materials and equipment.

recognition items
Test items presented generally in the form of a question or a declarative statement where the student is presented with alternative answer choices. Since the correct answer is listed the student must simply recognise the appropriate choice.

GLOSSARY OF TERMS — APPENDIX 1.

role play
Trainees are given information about a situation and are asked to perform as if they were involved in a real life event. A role play is one of the simplest forms of simulation training.

skill
A manipulative action performed while producing a finished product or performing a task. Also called an operation, task or competency.

standard
That part of a performance objective which describes how well or to what proficiency level a task must be performed. Also called a performance level, criterion, or work standard.

task
A discrete unit of work performed by an individual in the completion of an assigned job duty. Each task has a definite beginning and ending within a limited period of work time.

task analysis
A process that is executed in order to better understand job tasks. It involves breaking down the job tasks into consecutive steps or component parts. Once separated each element is analysed to determine its relative importance in terms of accomplishing the job task.

validation
A process used to determine if curriculum materials are as effective with the students as the developer intended them to be. Validation requires that the materials be presented to the students and data gathered relative to that use. Based on the results the curriculum is revised until it proves effective. Also a procedure used to determine and verify if tasks/competencies identified for a educational program are valid.

Index

APPENDIX 2

APPENDIX 2.

audience,	3, 25, 26, 93, 96, 116, 128, 130, 153, 211, 241 (see also course)
audio-visual materials,	104, 120, 148, 150-154 case study, 127-129 classroom,
classroom instruction,	114
conditions,	40, 42, 62, 69, 70, 78, 80, 81, 138, 184, 185
constructed response items,	167, 175-182
content,	4, 16, 19, 20, 28-31, 41, 43, 51, 54, 100, 101, 103, 105, 108, 141, 155, 191, 195-197
course:	audience, 5-17, 20-21 description, 16-18, 85, 92, 96, 98-99 evaluation, 93, 104, 162 objectives, 80, 81, 84, 94, 95, 100, 104, 210 outline, 92, 100-103 planning, 85, 92-98, 211, 241 purpose, 93 schedule, 93, 96-97, 211 title, 93, 210, 240
curriculum,	3, 4, 15-20, 25-27, 32, 39, 41, 46, 53, 54, 57, 62, 162, 191-199, 200, 202-203
curriculum development,	3, 4, 15-20, 25, 26, 28, 32, 39, 41, 42, 54, 57, 197-198, 201-202,
demonstration,	25, 87, 95, 104, 117, 123-125
developing a performance test,	179-185
discrepancy,	40

field demonstrations,	25, 117, 131-133
Food and Agriculture Organization,	3-5, 19, 25
gap analysis,	39-40, 43-49, 57-62
goals, instructional,	26
group discussion,	117, 121-122, 229-233
handouts,	31, 102, 229-233, 148 (see also training support materials)
instructor presentation,	117-120, 248
job analysis,	43-50
knowledge tests (see tests)	
learning, principles of,	16, 18, 31, 85-89, 165
lesson plan,	(see training plan)
measurement of learning,	162-163 (see also tests)
needs analysis,	39, 42-43, 57
needs assessment,	39
needs identification,	39, 40-42, 57

objectives:	67-68
	behavioural, (see performance)
	course, 194, 240
	training,18, 28, 68, 71, 79, 100, 134-135,196-197
	performance, 68, 80
organising content,	30, 90-91
performance,	28-29, 67, 69-81, 85, 186,
performance objectives, categories of,	73, 75-76, 80-81
performance verbs,	70, 73-77
performance tests,	(see tests)
phases of training,	26-32
preparing objectives,	134-135
principles of learning,	85-89, 167
problems,	4, 17, 42, 191, 195, 201
reading,	117, 125-126
recognition items,	167-174
role play,	117, 129-131
skill assessment,	102
standards,	69, 71-72
target audience,	(see also course)
task analysis,	51-56

tests:
    knowledge test items, 131, 161-164, 166-167, 171, 181, 184, 186, 191
        multiple choice, 167-169
        true false, 169-172
        matching, 172-174
        short answer, 175-177
        essay, 177-179
    performance test items, 166, 179-183, 185
        identification tests, 182-185
        work sample & simulatio, 182
        tests, 182
    test types, 164, 171, 173, 174, 176, 178-179, 192
    knowledge tests, 167-179
    performance tests, 182-185
    planning tests, 31, 164-166

training:
    content, 3-5, 25-27, 29-31, 39, 40-45, 50-51
    content outline, 88, 100
    gap, 40, 42
    materials, 27, 31- 32 (see training support materials)
    methods, 18, 27, 29, 30, 85, 88, 95, 103-104, 116-141
        selecting, 133-140
    need, 16, 18 26-28, 39, 42, 62, 67, 193
    plan, 18, 30, 92, 98-108, 242-247
    process, 17, 25, 28, 39
    support materials, 27, 31, 147-156
        printed matter, 148-150
        audio-visual materials, 150-152
        developing support materials, 152-155

verbs:
    for knowledge, 73
    for physical action, 74-75
    for feelings and attitudes, 77

Selected and Forthcoming FAO's Publications on Agricultural Extension, Training, and Education.

Swanson, Burton (ed.). *Agricultural Extension: A Reference Manual.*
Rome: Food and Agriculture Organization (FAO) of the United Nations, 1984.
(Also available in French, Spanish, Arabic, and Portuguese versions)

Oakley, Peter and C. Garforth. *Guide to Extension Training.*
Rome: Food and Agriculture Organization (FAO) of the United Nations, 1985
(Also available in French, Spanish, Arabic, and Portuguese versions)

FAO. *The Management of Agricultural Schools and Colleges.*
Rome: Food and Agriculture Organization (FAO) of the United Nations, 1985.
(Also available in French, Spanish, Arabic, and Portuguese versions)

Axinn, George. *Guide on Alternative Extension Approaches.*
Rome: Food and Agriculture Organization (FAO) of the United Nations, 1988.
(Also available in Spanish version)

FAO. *Report of the Global Consultation on Agricultural Extension.*
Rome: Food and Agriculture Organization (FAO) of the United Nations, 1990.
(Also available in French and Spanish versions)

Elliot, Sergio. *Distance Education Systems.*
Rome: Food and Agriculture Organization (FAO) of the United Nations, 1990.

FAO. *Make Learning Easier: A Guide for Improving Educational/Training Materials.*
Rome: Food and Agriculture Organization (FAO) of the United Nations, 1990.
(Also available in French and Spanish versions)

FAO. *Improving Training Quality: A Trainer's Guide to Evaluation.*
Rome: Food and Agriculture Organization (FAO) of the United Nations, 1991.
(Also available in French version).

FAO. *International Directory of Agricultural Extension Organizations.*
Rome: Food and Agriculture Organization (FAO) of the United Nations, 1991.

FAO. *Agricultural Extension and Farm Women in the 1980s.*
Rome: Food and Agriculture Organization (FAO) of the United Nations, 1993.

FAO. *Strategy Options for Higher Education in Agriculture: Expert Consultation Report.*
Rome: Food and Agriculture Organization (FAO) of the United Nations, 1993.
(Also available in Spanish version)

Wentling, Tim L. and R. M. Wentling. *Introduction to Microcomputer Technologies: A Sourebook of Possible Applications in Agricultural Extension, Education, and Training.*
Rome: Food and Agriculture Organization (FAO) of the United Nations, 1993.

Stringer, Roger and H. Carey.
Desktop Publishing: A New Tool for Agricultural Extension and Training.
Rome: Food and Agriculture Organization (FAO) of the United Nations, 1993.

Forthcoming Publications:

Ausher, Reuben et.al.
The Potentials of Micro-Computers in Support of Agricultural Extension, Education, and Training.
Rome: Food and Agriculture Organization (FAO) of the United Nations.
(in press, expected out in late 1993)

Adhikarya, Ronny.
Strategic Extension Campaign: A Participatory-Oriented Method of Agricultural Extension.
Rome: Food and Agriculture Organization (FAO) of the United Nations.
(in press, expected out in 1994)

Swanson, Burton (ed.). *Improving Agricultural Extension: A Reference Manual.*
Rome: Food and Agriculture Organization (FAO) of the United Nations.
(under preparation, expected out in 1995)

For more information on these publications, please write to:
Chief,
Agricultural Education and Extension Service (ESHE)
Human Resources, Institutions, and
Agrarian Reform (ESH) Division
FAO of the United Nations.
Via delle Terme di Caracalla
Rome 00100 - ITALY
Phone: (39 - 6) 5225 - 4001
Fax: (39 - 6) 5225 - 3152